# THE JUDAS MYSTERY

Religious and Moral Education Press
*An imprint of Chansitor Publications Ltd,*
*a wholly owned subsidary of Hymns Ancient & Modern Ltd*
*St Mary's Works, St Mary's Plain*
*Norwich, Norfolk NR3 3BH*

First published 1997

ISBN 1-85175-109-2

**Note**
Information on how this book can be used in schools is provided on
pages 105 to 107. Notes for Christian study groups appear on page 108.

Designed and typeset by Topics - The Creative Partnership, Exeter

Illustrations by Clive Wakfer

Printed in Great Britain by BPC Wheatons Ltd, Exeter
for Chansitor Publications Ltd, Norwich

# Preface

Detective stories set in the distant past are still fairly unusual, despite the success of the Brother Cadfael stories as books and television. The crime writer H. R. F. Keating calls such stories 'history with mystery'. A mystery set in the ancient world has its special problems for the reader and also the detective. Witnesses are dead. The scene of the crime has altered. The body isn't available to be examined. The written documents that survive don't always answer the questions we might want to ask centuries later. In the real-life case in this book, the story-line is mine but I've tried to make the details of the mystery as true to life as possible, using biblical books or other Christian writings to support the story, without at the same time assuming that even they are true in every detail. So this book is 'documentary history with mystery'.

The central question is simple: nearly everyone has heard of Judas, 'the traitor', but *was* he a traitor? What was he like? What exactly did he betray? How did he die? Was he any worse than Jesus' other friends, one of whom denied that he'd ever met him? Was Judas really bad at all? If so, why? Would we be sympathetic if we knew more about him? The answers aren't as simple as the questions, partly because the writers of the Christian gospels were interested in only the *fact* of Judas betraying Jesus, not the detail or background or motive.

I've used various sources for information: some of the New Testament writers as well as some of the books that weren't selected to go into the New Testament, in addition to the Jewish historian Flavius Josephus, and some second-century Christian writers. I've referred to books by modern scholars such as Schuyler Brown, Daniel-Rops, R. L. Harris, E. Hennecke, J. Jeremias and J. A. Thompson, whose writings helped me to reconstruct daily life in the times of the story and assisted my interpretation of the surviving ancient writings. I am also very grateful for advice from some members of the Theology Department at the University of Exeter, in particular Professor David Catchpole, Dr Alastair Logan and Donald Murray, in answer to specific questions I raised. All these people helped provide background for the case, but I claim full credit for any mistakes!

Mary Mears, the accomplished crime editor of my modern Mysteries Series, has stepped back into the past to edit this. Her sleuthing talents have not aged with the passing of two thousand years.

## A Note on Slavery

In the ancient world slavery was an accepted part of daily life. Even the Bible doesn't criticize it head on, though Paul as a leading Christian wrote that in a new sort of existence possible in Christ there would be neither slave nor free. To modern readers the word 'slave' rightly stands for an ugly and unacceptable state of human existence, ongoing in parts of the world today where people, often children, are still sold or made to work for little or no money in harsh conditions. The Anti-Slavery Society still has a job to do. Because the word 'slave' stands out so much now, yet was so ordinary and accepted then, I've used the Greek work for slave, *doulos*, in its other, equally correct translation as 'servant'. That makes the relationship look more matter of fact, as it would have been in the ancient world at the time.

T.C.

# THE JUDAS MYSTERY

## TERENCE COPLEY

RMEP

A MYSTERY FOR YOU! TO INVESTIGATE

# A Private Investigation

In this book, you, the reader, go back in time more than nineteen centuries and play the role of a private investigator employed by His Excellency Theophilus. Imagine the opening scene.

It's 30 degrees, but you're standing in a large, cool room, with marble pillars. You're wearing a loose-fitting robe and sandals. There's a gentle breeze wafting in from the deep-blue Mediterranean Sea, visible beyond the balcony. Your mind has drifted from the rather fat, cross, bald but very important man seated at a large table some distance away. He hasn't noticed you haven't been paying attention and continues talking:

'That man is a mystery. His life was mysterious and his death was mysterious. Now take me, for example – I'm an administrator. My job is to organize people and things, neatly, smoothly. I don't like mystery. I like answers and systems and solutions and things that fit. I want to close the file on this case. I want you to find out what happened. I want it solved, and I want it solved quickly.'

'Well,' you begin, 'it looks straightforward to me, Excellency.' Your wealthy employer pauses, holding the grape he was about to pop into his mouth in mid-air. His face goes redder.

'Straightforward? You call it straightforward?' He jumps up, dropping the grape, and walks across to the scroll cupboard. He takes out an armful of scrolls then dumps them on the table, with the grape splattered somewhere underneath. You know him well enough to guess that some sort of outburst will follow.

'Look at all these,' he splutters. 'No sooner had that new religion started than people tried to write accounts of it, to make sense of it. I've collected them. Paid a lot for them. They're neatly filed here in the cupboard. I even employed an agent myself, Luke. I thought an educated man like him, a doctor, would get to the bottom of it. He's gone off and retired – they say he's a painter these days – so he's not even

3

available to work on the problem. What's painting pictures going to solve? Eh?'

'What needs solving, Excellency?' You try not to make him lose his temper. 'The person you're enquiring about is dead, after all.'

'Of course he's dead. I know that!'

'They say he betrayed Jesus, the one at the centre of the new religion.'

'Well of course he did! Any passing idiot who knows the slightest thing about the new religion knows Jesus was betrayed by Judas. What interests me is why. What sort of man would do that to his friend?'

'Surely, Luke ...'

'Luke! Luke! Look here! Luke wrote two books, fair enough, dedicated them to me. But they left me wondering about Judas. He's hardly mentioned. Even Judas' death was odd. It's clear as mud what Luke meant in his second book when he said ... But why am I telling you all this? I don't want to tell you what I know. I want you to tell me what I don't know.'

'Didn't Judas commit suicide? I've heard somewhere. Isn't that what everybody says?'

'Everybody! What does everybody know about it? Why should a man commit suicide when he's achieved precisely what he set out to do? It makes no sense. Besides, Luke implied that the death was a nasty accident. But I said to myself: there are accidents and accidents. Get my meaning?' He glares, eyebrows raised. You nod, even if you don't get his meaning. You don't want him to throw those scrolls at you.

'So I want you to investigate this man Judas.'

'Er, what do you want in my report?'

'I want you to find out *what* Judas did, *why* he did it, *how* he died and any detail at all you can be sure about.'

'How shall I start to ...?'

'That's your business. That's what I'm paying you for. Just get on with it. Money isn't the issue. Use what it takes, but get me answers. I can write to my agents in the towns you visit and get them to release money as you need it.'

'But surely the army could look into ...'

4

'Why should it be a military matter? They've no interest in it. Judas was nothing to them.'

'Don't the Jews have some sort of security force?'

'Fool! Of course they *did*! There were the Temple police. But there haven't been any Temple police for more than twenty years. Not since the Empire destroyed the Jerusalem Temple.* When they did exist, the Temple police only concerned themselves with what went on in the Temple. Besides, they might have been involved in Judas' death, or some sort of cover-up afterwards. No, the only way of solving this is by private investigation. Just get on with it.'

'Yes, Excellency.' He's unrolling one of the scrolls he took out, using its wooden handles to move it to the place he wants. That's his way of telling you that you're no longer wanted and the interview is over. As you hesitate he adds,

'Keep careful notes. Write down what you might not remember. Weigh up the evidence. Is it reliable? What's possible? What's probable? What's certain? Remember, I want a clear report when you come back.' He pauses. 'Now get out! I've done half the job for you already!'

You hurry out, leaving Theophilus to his scroll before he can throw it at you. You nod to the soldier on guard outside the door as you go. He raises his eyebrows at you as if to say, 'Difficult man in there. You should see him on a bad day!'

---

* Theophilus is referring to the destruction of Jerusalem in 70 C.E., when the Jewish Temple was destroyed, the treasures looted and taken to Rome and the priests killed. The Temple has never been rebuilt and today only the Western Wall and part of the Temple platform remain.

# How You Investigate the Mystery

Your task is to collect information about Judas to put in a report for His Excellency Theophilus. There are several ways of unravelling this mystery and although you will be able to read about other people's solutions, you're challenged to produce one yourself that fits the facts. If you are using this book in a group rather than alone, you might compare and discuss your ideas as you work through it and try to agree a group solution.

Every few pages in this book, you are asked to choose what you, the investigator, do next. When you have decided what action to take or which line of enquiry to try, you go to another page and read on. As in real life, some choices will work out better than others. While you're trying to find answers for Theophilus, you'll have to watch out for possible dangers and delay. You must be careful:

• not to lose too many months on the enquiry,

• not to get arrested,

• not to end up dead!

At the time of this story an investigator would have remembered tiny details more easily than we can. Because there were no tapes, videos, computer disks or even exercise books for recording and storing information, people's memories were sharper. We only train ours at exam time, so you'll need a notepad to jot down names or other details about the mystery as you read. When you near the end of the book, you may want to write down possible solutions before making your final deductions – or guesses. It's also a good idea to have something you can use as a bookmark so that you don't lose your place, and to write down page numbers of important sections, so that you can find and read them again if you need to.

In your report for Theophilus, you will need to say:

• *what* Judas did,      • *why* he did it,      • *how* he died,

and give any detail at all you can be sure about.

Remember, Theophilus is obviously expecting reliable evidence, so you will have to weigh up carefully what people tell you and decide:

- Is it certain?
- Is it probable?
- Is it possible?
- Is it impossible?

You'll also have to ask yourself, 'How do I know?'

# How Much of This Book is True?

As you read on, you won't always be able to pick out fact and fiction easily. The openings of both of Luke's books are addressed to someone called Theophilus (although some scholars think he was invented by Luke to represent the general reader). However the conversation he has with the investigator – you! – is entirely fictitious and so is his personality as presented here. Julia, Paulus and Simon Barabbas – like you – are fictitious too. There was of course a real Judas, and trying to get at what 'really' happened to him is one of the aims of the story. But he could be any of the three Judases you later have the chance to investigate, or none of them.

The story background has been carefully researched to be real. The food, places and customs described are all historical fact: for instance, there really were biscuits made with ground locusts and they were seen as a treat.

Readers especially interested in the parts that are fiction and the parts that retell Bible accounts can find out more by looking up the Bible passages listed on page 104.

### References

At some points in the story there are asterisks that allow you to escape for a moment into modern times by turning to the list of references on pages 102 to 104. These references give you modern comments and information on remarks or events in the story that you might find puzzling.

# The Times You're Living In

Your investigation is taking place in the 16th Year of the Reign of the Emperor Domitian, the year your Christian servant Paulus calls the 95th Year of 'Our Lord'.* The Roman Empire controls most of the western world but times are unsettled. The Emperor favours people from outside Italy and has lost the support of the senators in Rome itself. They'd like to see him go. He's scared – with good reason – that they'll try to have him assassinated. So he's built up a massive spy network and anyone who questions him risks being charged with treason. He's already exiled a lot of the professors from Rome just because they criticized him. However, the army are fiercely loyal to him – he's given them a big pay rise. The ordinary people of Rome also like him because he seems to oppose those who lord it over them.

You're certain to meet at least one of the Emperor's spies on your travels so be on your guard. A careless remark or a choice on your journey that looks as if it's acting against the

* See also reference on page 102. Remember to bookmark this page so that you can return here quickly.

Emperor could lead to your arrest and worse. The Emperor regards Christians as 'atheists', because they don't believe in the Roman gods. So if you go around asking a lot of questions about these 'atheists' you won't be at all popular and you might end up dead.

Still, Domitian doesn't succeed in everything he does and even his paid 'ears' and informers can't be everywhere. It's rumoured that the army campaign to capture the distant Land of the Scots is going very badly.

Even sending Christian leaders like John the Theologian into exile on the remote rock island of Patmos can't stop their books being published. Apparently John's written a sizzling shocker called the Book of Revelation, which really does reveal all! It's said to be a mixture of horror and violence and a coded attack on the Emperor. But you don't know where to get hold of a scroll of it. It's much too risky to ask at the scribe factories where professional writers produce twenty, even fifty, copies of a book at a time under dictation from the scribe master. No one will risk paying them to produce that book! The scroll libraries in the universities won't dare stock it. So you'll have to keep an eye out for it on your travels if you want to read it.

Now read on. Good luck with your investigation!

# You prepare to set off on your investigation

You can't just rush off in search of the answer to this mystery. There are preparations to be made. You'll have to travel and that will mean months away from home.

First you visit your friends next door and explain that you're going away for some time. You ask if their servant will check your house every day and especially every night. You've seen those tell-tale holes through the plaster walls of houses when other people have been away! You don't want thieves to kick and break a hole into your house and take your best goods. So you pay cash now to your neighbour's servant to keep a good eye on the house, with the promise of treble that sum on your return if everything's safe and sound.

You get one of your own servants, Paulus, to sweep the floor carefully and leave everything neat. He re-lays the straw mats carefully after doing this. Perhaps if you find the solution to the mystery Theophilus will reward you and you'll be able to pay for a mosaic floor, or at least carpets, to replace those rather ordinary-looking mats.

You decide to take your two servants with you. They can do the detailed preparations, carry your luggage and help on the journey. It will be good to be free to work on the case without having to sort out meals and accommodation. Paulus has recently joined the new religion, 'the Way' as he calls it, so his knowledge could come in handy. Your other servant, Julia, will keep him in good order. She's very happy with the gods of Rome, so you might have to settle a good few arguments between the two of them on your travels.

When you're packed and ready, you decide to set off this afternoon, so that you've got four or five hours of daylight left to make a good start on your journey. The heat of the day is cooling. It's a good time to walk. You take your leave of the dark, strong-smelling living area of your house. There's no smell like home! You've already decided to leave

10

the animals where they are in the small courtyard. It will make it look as if you're at home and the servant at the nextdoor house on the other side will feed them while you're away.

'Oh – and if it rains heavily, don't forget to roller my roof as soon as you've done yours,' you tell the caretaking servant. Otherwise it might fall in.

You go up the outside stairs and onto the roof for a last look around. You check the low protection wall round the edge, required by law. Thanks to this, even old Uncle Annas didn't fall off when he slept up here on a visit, and he snores and rolls all over the place.

You wave to a neighbour who's putting out dates to dry on her roof. You call to another across the road who's sitting on her roof weaving. It makes you feel that with this neighbourhood watching, any thieving stranger in the village would soon be spotted. You feel better about leaving.

11

You've already been wondering about your route. Now you must decide where to go first:

- To begin your enquiries, you could consult a local Christian elder (their word for people who are senior or wise in this new religion). Paulus has given you the name of one of the elders in the large Christian group in the next village, eight kilometres away. You'd have to walk to the village then travel on from there, perhaps after an overnight stay. To take this route, turn to page 16.

- You could make straight for Jerusalem. That's where the new religion began, so it could be a good place to start your enquiries. To do this, you'll have to walk to the port and lodge there until you can catch a ship for Joppa on the coast of Israel. From there you can travel by road to Jerusalem. To take this route, turn to page 18.

Think: is it better to take more time and learn more at the start, by delaying your long journey slightly, or do you want to be off straight away? You have to choose between a delay now or setting off without information that may cause you longer delays later.

# You find out more about the disciples

'Who were these disciples? Where does Judas fit in?' you ask.

'Jesus had several groups of followers, friends,' Silas begins. 'In his gospel Luke talks about twelve men personally picked by Jesus but he also knew about another group of seventy men. He wrote that groups of women followers and friends were with Jesus as well. I can find you Luke's list of the twelve.'

After some shuffling through the pages he reads out the names from a different notebook: 'There was Simon Peter, his brother Andrew, James and John (they were brothers too), Philip, Bartholomew, Matthew, Thomas, another James (son of Alphaeus), another Simon (known as the Zealot), Judas son of James (but we don't know which James), and the Judas you're interested in, Judas Iscariot, the traitor.'

'It's a bit confusing, all those similar names.'

'It's more confusing still, because in other gospels the lists are slightly different.'

'How do you explain that?'

'Perhaps the writers said there were twelve because of the number symbolism, or perhaps some of them came and went and there were about twelve at any given time.'

'They must have had to go fishing to earn money sometimes,' says Paulus, looking at the practical issues. 'Some of them were fishermen before they were chosen by Jesus. He doesn't seem to have picked any farmers – perhaps they couldn't leave their crops to travel round with him. Or maybe it was because he mixed with fishermen while living at Capernaum by the Sea of Galilee. Maybe some went back to fish in Galilee while others carried on travelling with Jesus. That way they'd have had cash to live on while they went around preaching and healing.'

'What about Judas? What was his job?'

'He isn't described as a fisherman. Nobody bothered to write down what his job was, with him not being famous.'

'But aren't all these disciples famous to you followers of the Way?'

'Yes, but they weren't famous then, in the early days.'

'What more can you tell me about them? Are any alive now?

'Well, Simon Peter certainly isn't,' says Silas. 'It must be more than thirty years since he was crucified upside down in Rome in Nero's bad old days. Peter could have told you a lot.'

'I've heard tell John is still alive and living at Ephesus,' Paulus interrupts.

'Well, all I can say,' exclaims Silas crushingly, 'is that he must be a very old man now if he's alive at all.'

'But he could be alive! We could go and look for him,' Paulus suggests eagerly to you. 'After all, if he's alive we'll get the answer to the Judas mystery straight away. John would have known him. He was an eyewitness. He'll know what Judas did and how he met his death. It's about sixty years since Jesus was crucified. Thirteen is coming of age for Jews, so John could still be around. In his late seventies, eighties or nineties!'

'John wrote a gospel,' adds Silas. 'Why don't you try to get hold of a copy of that instead and save yourself the long journey to Ephesus?'

'We can't be sure John wrote one,' says Paulus, excitedly again. 'People are always claiming that famous people wrote the book they wrote. It's a way of getting the book noticed. Good publicity. The people who copy books sell more that way.'

'Do you have a copy of this gospel of John?' you ask Silas.

'I had the chance to buy one some years ago, but I couldn't afford it. Besides, I was more interested at the time in the one Matthew wrote.'

'The one they *say* Matthew wrote, according to you!' jokes Alexander to Paulus.

'Let's go and find John and ask him,' is his reply.

Now you joke back at him: 'If only people could fly like

14

the birds, I might pop and see John in a few hours! But we've got to be very sure before we go all the way to Ephesus in search of someone who's probably dead. It would take a long time. If we were still there in winter, sailing problems might add six months to the whole trip while we sat out the gales in Ephesus.'

'Take a chance! Go for it!'

But it's your choice, not your servant's. You think about it carefully. Your employer, Theophilus, wants answers. If you're delayed at Ephesus and try to sail back in winter, even if you can find a ship willing to take the risk, who's to say you'll arrive home safely? On the other hand, meeting John could solve questions that might take months to answer by other means. Ephesus is a famous city, worth seeing. One of the Wonders of the World is there.

Choose what to do next:

- Either hurry to page 18 and walk to the port, if you haven't already been there. At the port, you can catch a sailing for Joppa then walk on to Jerusalem. This would give you the chance to try to find out about Judas' death in the city where it happened.

- Or return to the port, if you have already been there, and sail to Joppa. To do this, go to page 26.

- Or go to Ephesus and try to talk to John, the last surviving disciple (if he *does* survive), to find out about Judas' life and death. To do this, go to page 22.

# You consult one of the Christian elders

First, Paulus has to convince Alexander, the Christian elder, that he can talk to you freely and that you aren't a government spy. Now that the new religion is seen as totally separate from the Jewish faith it grew up in, people are much more suspicious of it. Some Christians are being very cautious about talking too openly to strangers about it.

'I'm interested in Judas,' you say, to start the interview.

'Why?' Alexander answers you with a question, looking sharply at you.

'I want to know more about him – his life, his death.'

'"He was a member of our group, for he had been chosen to have a part in our work ... from which he turned aside, to go to the place where he belongs."' Alexander pauses impressively, as if you ought to understand this solemn remark. What does he mean? A member of our group? A part in our work? Turned aside? Where is 'the place where he belongs'?

'You seem to be speaking in riddles. I don't follow.'

'No riddles. I'm simply quoting what Luke said.'

'Luke? The one who was working for Theophilus?'

Alexander nods. That's at least getting you somewhere. You've stumbled on a Luke clue.

'Does Luke live around here?' you ask.

'Oh no. I don't know where he lives, or even if he's still alive, but that's what he said about Judas in his second book.'

'Is that all he said?'

'He said more in each of his books, actually.'

'Can I read what he said?'

Alexander chuckles. 'If you can read,' he replies.

You're rather offended by this. Does he imagine you're a peasant or low-ranking servant? Many servants can read and write, your own included. But Alexander ignores your annoyed look and continues: 'I don't own a copy of Luke-Acts but there is one in this village at the house of Silas.'

Do you want to visit Silas or abandon your enquiries here and set off for Jerusalem? To travel to Jerusalem, you'll have to walk to the port and lodge there until you can catch a sailing for Joppa on the coast of Israel. From there you can travel by road to Jerusalem.

- If you want to go to Jerusalem now, turn to page 18 and walk to the port, unless you went there before consulting Alexander.

- If you have already been to the port and want to return there to sail to Joppa, turn to page 26.

- If you want to go to the house of Silas and read what Luke said about Judas, turn to page 20.

# You walk to the port

At least you can attempt the trip to Joppa. It isn't the no-go sailing season, which lasts from November to mid-March. You're travelling in August – long live the memory of Caesar Augustus! This means that spring refits to the ships are over and the travel season is in full swing. In dock now there's a grain ship travelling empty from Rome via your port to Joppa to pick up grain for the capital, along with some choice dates and honey for export to the wealthier Romans. It will sail soon. The weather is good. The winds are strong, for fast sailing, but not too strong. The captain won't want to miss them.

The ship isn't too crowded as you're not travelling at the peak season for Jewish visitors, which is Passover time. Not that the visitor traffic is anything like it used to be in the days of the Jewish Temple in Jerusalem. Another advantage of good weather is that when you reach Joppa, you should have no trouble in joining a large group of travellers headed for Jerusalem, so you should be safe from robbers.

You moan to Julia that you're not particularly looking forward to sleeping on the deck on mats rented from the crew, or just with your cloak wrapped round you, especially

18

if there's lots of heavy rain or sea spray. Julia hasn't travelled by sea before.

'I expect I'll be sea sick,' she starts to complain.

'Well at least you won't have to eat the ship food then,' you answer. 'There'll be no bread – it goes mouldy too quickly.'

'So that's why you made me pack two days' supply of our bread and mint-flavoured flourcakes as well as all that dried salted fish!'

'Yes, and I've bought some special biscuits as a treat, made from locust powder. The locusts are boiled, their legs and head removed and bodies dried in the sun. Then they're ground down into powder, mixed with wheat flour and baked. We'll need the red wine we've brought in those two new tanned goatskins because ship water always tastes brackish and nasty. Mixed with water as usual, the wine will hide the horrible taste of the ship water, while the water will dilute the wine and make it a bit more thirst quenching.'

'What if we run out?'

'The captain will have plenty more wine – for a price. His will be scented with a choice of thyme, cinnamon or roses.'

Julia looks at the ships in the harbour. 'Do we have to sail today?'

'It's as good a time to travel as we'll get. I don't know how long the trip will take, but with the winds in the right direction, ten days or a fortnight at most should see us at Joppa.'

Choose what to do next:

- Either consult one of the Christian elders in a nearby village, if you haven't already done so, even if it delays your sailing. To do this, walk to page 16.

- Or risk sailing to Joppa and the road journey to Jerusalem. To do this, go to page 26.

# You go to the house of Silas

Silas must have been on his roof and seen you coming from some distance. He blocks the narrow entrance to his house suspiciously until he realizes that it is Paulus and Alexander the elder who are with you. Three people striding towards his house might be agents of the Emperor. He knows the other two, so his suspicion changes to a look of warm welcome.

'Of course, of course,' he says when he learns the reason for your visit. 'My copy of Luke-Acts is my most precious possession. We read from it in our worship. The services take place here in my house. You're always welcome. Every Sunday at sunrise. Then we breakfast together and all go off to work.' So that's why your servant Paulus gets up and goes out so early on Sundays. You smile politely without actually agreeing to go to one of these dawn events and watch Silas go to a cupboard built into the wall. To your surprise he takes out a set of notebooks.

'The scroll copies are too fiddly – each nearly ten metres long, you know. It's hard to find a passage, and they can easily be damaged. So I paid to have codex copies made.* Just in case the state turns against us and we're ever arrested, the two scrolls for Luke-Acts are ... let's say

* See also reference on page 102.

in a safe place somewhere.' He winks and starts turning the pages to find the part that interests you.

'Here it is,' he says, and passes the open book to you. You read:

> ... Peter stood up to speak. 'My fellow Christians,' he said, 'the scripture had to come true in which the Holy Spirit ... made a prediction about Judas, who was the guide for those who arrested Jesus. Judas was a member of our group, for he had been chosen to have a part in our work.

With the money that Judas got for his evil act he bought a field, where he fell to his death; he burst open and all his bowels spilt out. All the people living in Jerusalem heard about it, and so in their own language they call that field Akeldama, which means "Field of Blood".'

You pause, putting the notebook down. Silas explains, 'Luke goes on to say they elected a disciple to replace Judas. There were two candidates, Joseph Barsabbas and Matthias. Matthias was elected. They couldn't have both, because of trying to keep the symbolic number twelve.'

'Twelve?'

'The twelve tribes of old Israel.'

'But what about Judas?'

'He fades out of the story. He was held to have resigned from being a disciple by his actions and to have gone to his own place.'

'What actions?'

'Betraying the Lord.' You look blank. 'Jesus,' he adds in explanation.

'Was Judas' death an accident?' you ask. 'Could he have been pushed?'

'Who knows?' Silas shrugs his shoulders. 'But of course when Luke said "he fell", his words could equally mean "he swelled up".'

'You mean he suffered a terrible illness and sort of burst?'

'Yes. But it's all the same in the end, isn't it? He's dead.'

But is it all the same? Theophilus has asked you to dig deeper than this. You think of the key words: 'possible', 'probable', 'certain'. Do any apply here?

Choose what to do next:

• Either hurry to page 18 and walk to the port if you haven't already been there. At the port, you can catch a sailing for Joppa then walk on to Jerusalem. This would give you the chance to try to find Akeldama, the Field of Blood.

• Or return to the port, if you have already been there, and sail to Joppa, by going to page 26.

• Or delay here a little longer to find out more about the disciples, by going to page 13.

21

# You go to Ephesus

You disembark at Miletus harbour, about five kilometres from Ephesus, and join the large crowd of new arrivals walking to the town. Docking wasn't easy. River silt has been a problem at Miletus for years and your ship was so heavily loaded with grain that it nearly grounded.

On the outskirts of Ephesus you are pestered by people who want to show you round and take you to the temple of Artemis, one of the Wonders of the World, or sell you souvenirs, cheap statues of Artemis in clay or expensive ones in silver. Magicians and fortune-tellers have stalls along the road. Julia wants to look. You notice an inscription on a building: 'If the bird flies from right to left, and settles out of sight, good luck will come. But if it lifts its left wing, it brings bad luck.' Do you believe in luck?

The road goes right past the theatre, which a guide says seats 25 000. It's a marble paved road, with colonnaded shops to keep shoppers and traders cool in summer and dry in the rains.

Paulus finds it's easy to contact Ephesus Christians as there are various large groups. It seems almost anyone can tell you the name of some Christian person or group to contact. An hour later you're sitting with a group of curious Ephesian Christians and some good food. They want to know all about your journey, what's happening in your home town, why you've come, whether you know anyone they know, and how it is with the Way, their name for the new religion, where you live. It's some time before you can question them and their leader, Festus. His first replies are disappointing.

'There's no John the disciple alive here now. I never met him if he was here, but then I came from the country to find work about ten years ago. There are Christians who say that he lived here and that he brought the Lord's mother here to live with him. I've even seen a house they say she lived in. But who knows?

'Then there's a story that John the disciple ran out of the

public baths down the main street naked and soaking wet as a protest when Cerinthus – a great enemy of the Way – jumped into the water. John didn't want to share the water with him! But I can't be sure that isn't gossip. You so often talk to someone who knows someone who's seen it, but never to anyone who's seen it first hand!

'I can't even tell you for sure whether John's buried here. There are several tombs of John in the city: John the elder, another John and perhaps John the disciple, but who can tell? There are lots of Christian groups in a city as big as this and we don't know all of them well. You've got to be careful,' he lowers his voice, 'the way things are.'

Several of the group stare harshly at Julia, who's made it quite clear that she's not a member of their religion and doesn't want to be. They obviously fear she's a government spy. But it doesn't stop Festus continuing, 'What we do have is a copy of the recent gospel. It was certainly written in this area and it's got information not in the others. It's known as the Gospel of John.'

'But did John write it?' you persist. He shrugs his shoulders.

'Does it matter? Or does it matter more that it contains truth?'

'Does it mention Judas?'

'Oh yes. It names his father, Simon Iscariot. One of our people has a copy that calls him Simon from Kerioth*, but the other copies we've seen just say Iscariot, so one of the scribes must have made a mistake copying – or a deliberate "improvement" to the gospel.

'The Gospel of John also says Judas was the treasurer and looked after the disciples' money when they were travelling round. It says he objected strongly when Jesus was anointed with expensive perfume by his friend Mary. (Don't confuse her with his mother Mary!) It says the perfume used was nard. If it was the real thing, it would have come from India, so it's not surprising that Judas said it was worth a working person's wage for a year. He probably wasn't exaggerating. Judas went on to say that the money should have been given to the poor instead of used as ointment for Jesus. But he said this, according to this gospel, not out of care for the poor, but because he was busy stealing what was in the disciples' common fund.'

'Well, I suppose it would make him out to be a thief, wouldn't it? Poor Judas. You Christians must have been really keen to blackwash him and make him out a criminal. I feel sorry for him.'

---

* See also reference on page 102.

---

There's a stunned silence. The speaker is Julia. As a non-Christian she obviously feels some sympathy for the way Judas has been treated in this recent gospel. You glare at her. She's clearly offended your new friends. She lapses into silence, but continues to frown her disagreement.

'The gospel also says that none of the disciples guessed that Judas was the traitor,' Festus continues. 'Peter only knew because Jesus gave him a private signal, by passing a piece of bread to Judas at their last meal. After that, the gospel says that Satan entered Judas and he left the room to arrange the arrest of Jesus.'

'Does it say what happened to him after the betrayal?'

'No. Nothing about that. I've told you everything it says about Judas.'

It's not what you hoped for. You haven't met John the disciple. But you have heard new things about Judas. You'll have to keep Julia quiet when you're interviewing Christians in future.

You can spend the night here. Miletus is such a busy port you'll be almost certain to catch a sailing out this week, perhaps even tomorrow. Maybe you'll be able to fit in a visit to the theatre first. There's a comedy on by Publius Terentius Afer, Terence for short. It's called 'The Mother-in-Law'. Julia's very keen to go and see it, as Terence was a servant who became a freeman and famous writer. His plays have a gentle, dry humour and often involve a mix-up between couples. You've heard the plot of this one. At the beginning, a wife and husband separate quite quickly after their marriage, supposedly because of the mother-in-law. But in the twists and turns of the plot the mother-in-law turns out to be the goody and the baddie who the husband is trying to discover is neither her not his wife ...

- If you haven't been to Jerusalem, get ready for the theatre then prepare to sail to Joppa and walk to Jerusalem, by turning to page 26.

- If you have been to Jerusalem, return to page 88.

25

# You sail to Joppa

Two weeks later, thinner than you were, you're looking down on Jerusalem from a hill across the valley. Walking from Joppa with lots of people has kept you safe and the ship food and heavy rolling of the sea are far enough behind to joke about, rather than make you feel sick.

Julia and Paulus have been good company, although Paulus kept praying to his invisible god and Julia went out of her way to offer incense to any other god's statue she passed at the port. This caused big rows between them. At least in this Jewish land there are no statues of gods. The people believe that statues are against the will of their invisible god. One of their Ten Rules forbids making them.

You stare at the men of this country. According to Jewish custom they have long beards, mostly untrimmed. It's a contrast with the clean-shaven Roman style you're used to seeing. You wonder what these strict Jews would say if they could see the trendy rich young men in your town with their hair sprinkled with gold dust. Not many Jewish women dye their hair with the Antioch-red or henna women in your town use. Here they plait it, sometimes piling it on top of the head like Roman women do, but without Roman ribbons and head ornaments.

You were pestered at Joppa by people trying to sell you good-luck charms: a locust's egg, a fox's tooth, a nail said to have been used for a crucifixion. Julia bought herself a crescent-moon pendant and a small pot of rouge with some antimony for eye shadow, black for the brows and blue for the lashes. Paulus frowned and told her this was extravagance.

Some of the men and women here obviously use scent in fairly large quantities. When you asked a shopkeeper why, he winked and told you that it's better than sweat in this hot climate. You treated yourself to some cinnamon scent. It smells better than the alternative he offered you – camphor.

Jerusalem isn't at all what you expected. You have read a

famous book by Flavius Josephus called *The Jewish War*. He said the whole place was destroyed twenty-five years ago and that 'the fortifications around the city were so completely levelled to the ground that no-one visiting the spot would believe it had once been inhabited'. The walls and forts *have* been demolished, so they can't be used in another war against the Romans, and the great Temple, jewel of the Jewish religion, has gone almost completely. All that's left is a foundation wall of the platform area, at which Jews can mourn and pray. But there are still houses and inhabitants. Some houses must have been built since the war but some might have survived from before then. Maybe Josephus exaggerated.

In the distance you can see by the road a sight you don't relish passing: ten or a dozen crosses, four with bodies on. Two Roman guards – you can tell by the uniform – are squatting on the ground looking at the earth between them, probably playing a dice gambling game. You can't see exactly

from where you are, but the fact that they are there means that one at least of the people crucified must still be alive.

'I wonder what they've done,' says Paulus.

Julia's eyesight is better than yours. She sees that one figure is attached with the front of the body facing the cross, back to any onlooker. 'A woman!' she exclaims.

You pause at this distance, not really wishing to approach nearer. However one of the local people overtakes you on the road. She sees you looking ahead.

'Ah!' she says, pointing towards them grimly. 'Zealots.'

'Terrorists who're trying to push Rome out,' explains Julia. 'Don't they ever learn, these Jews?'

'Ask this woman how to get to the place where Judas died,' prompts Paulus.

'We're looking for the place where Judas died,' you ask. The woman stares at you blankly.

'She won't know about Judas,' says Julia.

'Luke's book says the place was known as the Field of Blood,' adds Paulus. The woman turns and stares equally blankly at him. Julia solves the problem for you:

'Don't you speak Greek here? I thought the whole world spoke Greek. "Zealot" is a Greek word. She recognized that.'

'Yes, but "terrorist" is a useful word to know if you want to stay alive! Everyone knows "zealot". I'll talk to her in Latin,' you say, proud of your education in the language of the Roman upper classes. But the stranger still stares back at you.

'I gather most of them do speak Greek here,' adds Paulus, 'but the local language is called Aramaic. Luke mentioned the Aramaic name for the Field of Blood in his book. Let me try to remember it: Akel something ... yes, Akeldama!'

This time the woman's face lights up. 'Ah,' she exclaims, 'Akeldama,' and waves with her hand for you to follow her.

You leave the road, by-passing the crucifixion site, but near enough to see that according to custom the victims are naked, which is why the woman has been crucified facing the stake. One of the victims at least is trying to say something. You look away and hurry after the woman.

The path takes you through a field of sheep. You nod to the shepherd, noting with some surprise that a number of

the sheep have one of their back legs tied to their tail. The shepherd sees you looking curious and guesses this isn't a custom in your country. He can speak Greek well enough, for he calls out,

'Those are the ones that keep running off. I don't want Mr Jackal or Mr Wolf to get them, so I've slowed them down a bit.' He walks with you, followed by two very tame sheep, to whom he occasionally turns and talks in Aramaic. They nuzzle up to him whenever he slows enough for them to catch up. He wants to know what you're doing there and you explain your interest in Judas and his death.

'The Christian Jews were around here until the War*,' he spits, indicating his feelings about them, 'but now we expel

* See also reference on page 102.

anyone from the synagogue who claims to be a Christian Jew.'

'I'm a Christian but not a Jew,' explains Paulus. The shepherd stares at him.

'I've nothing against *you*,' he says, 'as such. It's the Christian Jews who are not true to our religion. They should give up being Jews altogether if they want to follow a blasphemer who was nailed up for treason.' Paulus has the sense to shut up.

You walk on and leave the shepherd behind. It isn't until you've left his field that it occurs to you that he's been walking along with you to make sure you aren't a sheep-thief. A sheep-thief indeed! But your other guide is leaving you now. She points to the area ahead of you. 'Akeldama,' she says, and is gone.

'Remind me what Luke wrote about Judas,' you tell Paulus, trying to remember a conversation on the journey here.

'"He bought a field, where he fell to his death: he burst open and all his bowels spilt out ... They call that field Akeldama, which means Field of Blood."'

'It's just as likely to mean "Field of Sleep", a cemetery,' says a voice behind you. 'You've not been told the full story, not at all.' You jump and turn round to see a man aged at least thirty-five with grey hair and a long beard. He carries a rather threatening wooden staff, either to lean on as he walks, or as a defensive weapon.

'I hear,' he goes on in rather bad Greek, with what you assume is a strong Aramaic accent, 'that you want to know about Akeldama. Well here you are and here I am.'

'Who are you?'

'Jacob. I'm the cemetery-keeper.' He holds his hand out. You're expected to give him a coin. But before you can decide whether you'd be wasting your money or whether you won't learn anything unless you pay, you hear a shout from across the field.

'They're over there! Arrest them immediately!' You can tell by the uniform that it's a Roman centurion with about twenty soldiers, advancing across the field towards you with drawn swords.

30

'Quick,' says Jacob, 'there's no time to lose. Come with me!' He turns to run away from the soldiers.

You have to choose:

- Either to run with Jacob, hoping that you can escape and then find out what information he has. To do this, go to page 41.
- Or to be bold and face the centurion, explaining that you're nothing to do with Jacob. To do this, go to page 32.

If you face the centurion, there's a risk that he will not believe you and will arrest you. On the other hand if you run and the soldiers catch you, it will look as if you're guilty of something and that could be worse. Remember that you're trying to avoid time-wasting, arrest and death!

# You face the centurion

'This way,' you say, turning to Julia and Paulus, trying not to appear scared.

The soldiers, swords in hand, are running fast towards you, but they draw back in surprise when they see you're walking towards them without weapons. You decide to call out in your best Latin accent 'Pax', which means 'Peace'. They look slightly less hostile and those nearest to you actually run on past in an attempt to capture Jacob. The others surround the three of you, pin your arms behind you and roughly march you off to face the centurion. He's a young officer, and when you see him closely, rather nervous-looking.

'At least we've got three of you,' he announces, relieved. 'That should please the Governor.'

'It all depends,' you answer as calmly as you can, 'who you think we are and if you know what you're doing.'

'Don't think you can lie your way out of this!' he snaps, more anxious than confident. 'You're zealot terrorists. That's who you are. And you're going to meet three nice crosses to die on for your trouble.'

'Listen,' you answer, still trying to sound bold, 'before you make a serious mistake that costs you your job. Did you ever see a terrorist with two servants? Or unarmed? Or with papers in his purse from his Excellency Theophilus, employing us in his service? Did you ever meet a Jewish terrorist who was a Roman citizen from abroad and spoke good Latin?'

The centurion looks very unsure now, and replies, 'I bought my Roman citizenship for a large sum of money.'

'Well,' you answer slightly pompously, 'I was born a Roman citizen, and as you very well know, that gives me all sorts of legal rights, including appeal to Caesar himself if idiots like you arrest me wrongly.' You stare hard at him.

'Actually,' you continue, 'I'll settle for an audience with the Governor here for a start. I can ask him what he thinks about your stupid action.' The soldiers who were chasing Jacob have arrived back panting, without him.

'Too quick for us, sir, and he knew the area too well. They can hide in shadows, these men.'

The centurion turns to you, this time as a friend: 'This urban terrorism is always bursting out,' he says. 'Please accept apologies based on my best intentions. I thought that ...'

'No harm done,' you reply, as the soldiers release the three of you. 'Let me show you my papers.' You produce your letter of commission from Theophilus. The centurion flicks through it, but he's obviously more concerned about capturing real terrorists.

'Know this country well?' he asks. You shake your head.

'Ever since the occupation, way back under General Pompey, they've been using hit squads to eliminate top Roman officials, or to attack trading convoys and steal the money to finance their rebellions, or to kill Jews who are prepared to co-operate with us. They even killed one of their own high priests once. They work in gangs. The Dagger Men were the worst. They used to carry small daggers hidden in their clothing and mix with crowds in the market-place. Then – swish – a silent plunge, three or four knives into their target. Before we could arrest them they'd be lost in the crowds. They'd never give up, those Sicarii.

'We catch a few terrorists, now and again, because we offer good rewards for the leaders, more than a slave's ransom. Then we nail them up for all to see, but it only makes the rest more fanatical. They've even sent armed gangs to try to rescue their crucified friends – we've had to increase the guard at executions ...'

You notice he's called the Dagger Men by their Latin name, Sicarii, because they each carried a *sicar* or small dagger. You also picked up in Joppa when you first arrived the common local word 'ish', meaning 'man of'. You're thinking about Judas. Could he have been Ish-Sicarii, 'Iscariot', a man of the Dagger Men? A member of the élite terrorist squad? The centurion won't know. He's not local, just stationed here with the army.

'What's this field?' you ask him.

'The locals call it Akeldama. It was used to bury foreigners who died while visiting Jerusalem. Somebody gave the money to buy it.' You look at the small, whitewashed stones around you: they're grave-markers.

'I'll tell you this,' adds the centurion, noticing you looking at the stones. 'No respectable Jews come here except for burials. It's religiously unclean. They even paint the tombs white so they don't walk on them by mistake. They don't use coffins. Relatives just wash the corpse, close its eyes, wrap it in a cloth, put some perfumes on, carry it here on a stretcher and bury it – all within eight hours of death.

'You should hear the row at funeral processions! They pay professional mourners to yell out "Alas, alas, Julius", or whatever the name of the dead person is! They cry, shriek, rub dust in their hair and they wear sack-cloth – all ritual. They even have to make a ritual tear in their clothes, not very big – it can be mended afterwards!

'The Jews bury their dead anywhere, as long as it's a minimum distance from a building. It's uncivilized. The only real cemeteries are for foreigners. By Jupiter, when you think about our fine Roman funeral stones! But in this country,' he sneers, 'graveyard-keeper's one of the lowest jobs you can get.

'Since no respectable Jews come here except for funerals, it's become a hang-out for zealots. We've been watching it. Take my advice – don't come here again. It's too dangerous. If they see you chatting to me, they'll think you're an informant and you could become a target.'

He turns to his men, 'Fall in! At the double!' They fall into marching line and start to move away. You feel strangely nervous about being left here and call to the centurion as he moves off,

'How can I contact Christians round here?'

'Try the Mount of Olives. Down that road,' he points to a road running away from the far end of the field. 'That's where the carpenter was arrested. They visit it to remember.'

'Let's go. I don't want to stay here.' It's Julia.

You must decide:

- Whether to visit the Mount of Olives, by going to page 38.

- Whether to stay here and see if you can find Jacob again, by going to page 36.

35

# You stay at Akeldama

'So this is the Field of Blood, bought with the money that Judas was paid to betray Jesus.' Paulus finds his voice again now that the soldiers have gone.

'What did he do to be paid that much money? Why didn't they just arrest Jesus themselves?' asks Julia.

'He must have shown them how it could be done quickly and quietly, at night, when the crowds weren't around. The crowds liked Jesus. After the way they had cheered him into Jerusalem in a big procession earlier that week, on the Sunday, they might have tried to rescue him and caused a riot at least, a full-scale rebellion at worst.'

'The way I heard it they were soon enough yelling for his death. Anyway, that's what crowds are like. One minute on your side, the next against. Listening to the centurion made me feel things can't have changed much in terms of uprisings and terrorism. Sometimes you think that even the mighty Roman Empire is only just hanging on to this bit of its lands,' says Julia. 'Where did they arrest your Jesus, then?'

'At the Mount of Olives, in the garden called Gethsemane.'

'Was he hiding there?'

'No. He'd gone there to pray. Judas arrived with torches, lights and armed men, kissed him as the signal and then he was arrested.'

'*Kissed* him?'

'A token kiss on the cheek, like they all do in this country. Jewish pupils used to greet their rabbis – religious teachers – like that. So Judas was greeting his religious teacher in the usual way. It wasn't odd.'

'I'm glad I never had to kiss the man who taught me to read!' is Julia's reply.

While they're chatting you are looking carefully around. There's no sign of Jacob. He must think it's too risky to return yet. But there's a young man, wearing a new white robe, or a newly washed one, watching you from some

distance away. Who is he? A curious local person? A government spy? A terrorist? Or a wandering possessed person*? You bravely stride towards him, but he's off down the lane and disappears.

You might as well visit the Mount of Olives on page 38 to try to make contacts there.

* See also reference on page 103.

# You visit the Mount of Olives

You follow the directions you've been given and arrive at the fairly obvious Mount of Olives. Running along a hillside facing what's left of the city wall is a small wood of olive-trees, some obviously old. The trees have low trunks and wide spreading branches, easy to hide among.

'The last night of Jesus' life was a Thursday and he seemed to know what was going to happen,' explains Paulus. 'After he finished his final meal with his friends he left the house, walked towards the Mount of Olives and into a garden called Gethsemane.'

'Geth what again?' asks Julia.

'In their language it means something to do with an oil press. With all these olives around some local business would have been using it, but not at night. Jesus was arrested at the time of full moon.' You imagine the shadows cast by the trees in moonlight.

'He must have been brave to face certain death,' you add.

'In a way not, because he prayed here that if possible he should be saved from a terrible death, but he also committed himself to the purposes of God. His prayer was "Not my will but yours be done".'

'Good job he had friends at a time like that,' says Julia.

'Actually, the few who were with him fell asleep while he was praying. He was facing death entirely alone. Apart from God.'

It's chilly. You shiver slightly as you imagine the desolation of the scene. Julia doesn't sense this atmosphere at all and adds loudly, 'Jesus must have been nutty not to run for it while he could. It would have been easy in the dark.'

But you're thinking about the arrest. Into this garden, somewhere near where you are, came Judas with armed men to arrest Jesus. What did Judas expect to happen? Perhaps that Jesus would be taken and crucified, exactly as it turned out. But if so, why do some people think that Judas committed suicide afterwards? Why should he regret a series of events that had gone according to plan?

On the other hand, suppose they did not go according to plan at all. What if Judas was a zealot like that other disciple, the Simon who wasn't Simon Peter? What if he had expected his friend Jesus to resist arrest and start an armed struggle that would begin in this quiet garden and end as a war that would drive the Romans out of the country altogether? What if Judas thought he was almost doing Jesus a favour, forcing him to attack the Romans? If that was the case, it could well explain why he committed suicide afterwards.

The trouble is, there are too many 'ifs' to be sure. *If* Judas was a zealot, or a sympathizer, *if* he thought Jesus would resist arrest, *if* he committed suicide and didn't die in an accident. And *if* all these ifs are correct, why did he set up the arrest when the crowds weren't around to join in an uprising? ... A distant cockcrow brings your mind back to the garden. You can't stand around thinking about this all day. As you're wondering what to do next you see Jacob approaching, with armed men. What's happening now? First soldiers run at you, now it's terrorists.

'Oh it's you again!' Jacob says. 'Now's your chance if you want to come on a raid. You can meet more zealots and maybe get your questions about Judas answered.'

Going with Jacob would be dangerous, but might help you meet key people. As you're deciding whether it's worth the risk, you notice a young man watching from behind an olive-tree. He's wearing a new white robe. Have you seen him before? Who is he?

Choose quickly:

- To set off on the raid, go to page 44.
- To follow the young man in white, go to page 40.

# You follow the young man

As you turn and head quickly towards the young man, he realizes that he's been spotted and makes a run for it. Now it's three after one. Paulus shouts:

'Leave him to me. Don't forget my athletic training.'

You remember he had a servant friend who worked at the stadium at home and who used to arrange for him to run there when it wasn't in use. That was in the hottest time of day, so it was good training. Paulus can certainly sprint quickly. He's soon left you and Julia behind. Soon after, he's out of sight round a bend. By the time you round the corner, he's lying on the ground, tangled in a white cloth. There's no sign of the young man.

'Are you all right?' you ask anxiously.

'Fine,' he pants, 'but our friend got away. We had quite a struggle.' He unravels the white cloth. It's the robe the young man was wearing.*

'He parted company with his clothing,' laughs Paulus, 'so he'll be a bit more obvious than we are.'

You look around. Obvious? He's nowhere in sight. Who is this young man? One of the Emperor's agents? A terrorist?

You've no option but to rejoin Jacob and set off on the raid.

Go to page 44.

---

* See also reference on page 103.

# You run with Jacob

'Keep up! Keep up!' he calls as you sprint away from the approaching soldiers. You can hear their armour rattling as they run behind you and a glance over your shoulder shows that they are carrying drawn swords. Suddenly you start to wonder what it must be like to be pierced by a sword. Do you feel terrible pain? Or just numbness? Wondering about it makes you run faster.

You're out of the field now, running down a road and past small houses. Jacob clearly knows what he's doing because he takes you down alleyways and round corners, through two houses and out on the other side. Gradually you realize that the only sounds are the four of you gasping for breath, with no clatter of armour from the pursuers any more. Jacob suddenly stops and knocks at a door, which is opened by a man with a small dagger in his hand. A glance behind shows your pursuers haven't caught up, but a young man in a white robe is watching you from a doorway opposite.

The man at the door Jacob knocked on motions you all in and the door is closed. You gradually accustom yourself to the dim light from the single oil-lamp burning in a niche in the wall in front of you. It's a poor house, because there are only rugs to sit or lie on plus some small square wooden stools with woven tops. They obviously can't afford chairs and the wooden table is a plain, low one, which means that

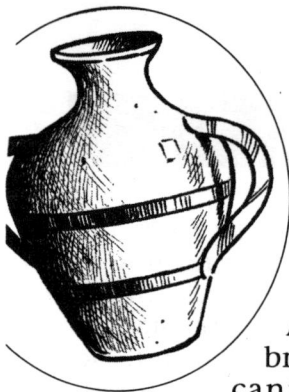

people will recline on the rugs to eat from it. You don't mind the lack of chairs. You're very glad to lie down on a rug after the chase and get your breath back.

A two-handled drinking flask is passed round and you take a long drink. There's nothing like fresh cool water from a well! After that you tuck into a hunk of barley-bread from a heavy, filling, round loaf. They can't afford wheat bread here, but barley's welcome all the same. It's still fresh and there's a small salad to go with it: cucumber, onion, olives, leeks, along with some lentils. These are really to add flavour to the bread and not themselves the meal. There's also salted fish, but you wait to take some of that until you've had more water to quench your thirst. When Jacob brings in a melon cut into chunks to eat with all this you feel it's been almost a banquet. He's joined by a woman who, like him, is in her early thirties.

'Meet Ruth, my wife,' he says, adding proudly, 'we've been married for nearly twenty years, since she was twelve and I was fourteen. Even then I was a member of the brotherhood. I've lost two sons fighting for it and I've two in it now. The daughters,' he laughs, 'I'm looking for good husbands for them! One's already betrothed, contracted to marry. For us, betrothal lasts about a year. It's a solemn as marriage – you can't break it without legal and cash penalties. The couple can't live together during betrothal, but if a child were to be born,' he winks, 'it would be a legal, legitimate child. I arranged my daughter's betrothal with the lad's father. I've known him for years.' He grins. You're feeling relaxed and glad to be away from the soldiers, but also uncertain about your host. And who was the young man watching in the street?

'Who *are* you? What brotherhood are you on about?' you ask your host.

'We're zealots. *They* call us terrorists. But ever since those swine* took God's Holy Land we've been determined to get it back, by force if necessary. Judas the Hammer, Judas the Galilean (not your Judas), the people of Masada, and lots more like them, are our heroes. Even the Jewish writer Flavius Josephus – the traitor took a Latin name but his real name's Joseph ben Mattathias – even he calls us "the Fourth Philosophy". He has to admit we're the fourth most important group in the land. You can't get far without our support.'

He looks at Paulus and continues, 'One of your Jesus' disciples was a zealot called Simon – not the famous Simon Peter, but another Simon. There are lots of us. We'll never give up until the Romans give up and go away. For every man they kill, two will spring up to take his place.'

The man who opened the door comes into the room. 'Time,' he announces.

Jacob turns to you. 'Come with us,' he says, 'join us on God's side against the forces of darkness.'

'What do you mean?' you ask.

'It's a raid,' he explains. 'Come with us.'

'Why?'

'Share our cause. And meet Simon.'

'The disciple who was a zealot?'

'No. This Simon is the son of Jesus Barabbas, the prisoner who was released at the Passover time when your Jesus was crucified.'

'Let's go and meet him! He might have information we need.' It's Paulus urging you to do this.

'Let's go and do anything rather than that! Do you want to die before your time? You haven't even made a protection offering to the great god Mars*.' It's Julia urging you not to go. 'Why don't we go to the Mount of Olives, the place where Jesus was arrested?' she suggests. 'Ruth's been telling me that Christians go there to remember.'

You must choose:

- Whether to set off on the zealot raid, by turning to page 44.

- Whether to visit the Mount of Olives and try to meet Christians there, by going to page 38.

---

* See also reference on page 103.

---

# You set off on the raid

Keeping to the shadows, you jog along the road with Jacob and his comrades.

'Where are we going?' you whisper to Jacob.

'The Jericho road. There's a merchant convoy moving up to Jerusalem. It's a very steep climb for them. We can conceal ourselves in the hills near the top, then when they're tired near the summit, we can move out and attack them.'

'Won't they be guarded?'

'Of course. But we'll be ready for the guards.'

You wonder. 'We' aren't in armour, nor are 'we' trained soldiers like the Roman army. But surprise will be on the side of the zealots, who'll not have had the slow tiring climb from the Jericho/Judaean desert end of the road. Julia has come with you and you notice that there are other women among the zealots. You ask Jacob about this.

'Why not?' says Jacob. 'Women feel about the cause like the men and having them with us helps us to be less noticeable when we're on the move. There were women at Masada* who were every bit as heroic as any man! Hang on! Here's the Simon you want to talk to.'

Out of the shadows, as it seems, you're joined by a very well-built man, carrying a short sword in one hand and a dagger in the other. Jacob explains to him who you are. He motions you to one side.

'We'll catch the others up easily. They're going to have to sit and wait for at least an hour, maybe several hours,' he explains. 'My father was around in Jerusalem at the time of the Judas you're interested in. Father was Jesus Barabbas and he was in a Roman dungeon!'

'Jesus like the other Jesus?'

'Sounds a bit of a coincidence? Not really. Yeshua in

---

* See also reference on page 103.

44

Aramaic – Jesus to you in Greek – was the most common
boy's name then. So releasing one Jesus in exchange for
another wasn't surprising. But the surname was.'

'How do you mean?'

'Well, in Aramaic, "bar" means "son of" and "abba"
means "father". So you see the man those Christians –
you're not one are you? – the man they call Jesus the Son of
God was crucified, but the man whose name means Jesus
Son of the Father was set free.'

'Have you heard it said that the other Jesus – not your
father – was raised from the dead?'

'Hmmph,' he snorts, 'well, I've seen a lot of men – and
some women – crucified. Some take it well; some take it
badly. Some take a long time to die. Some don't. They say
that other Jesus took only six hours, not long at all really.
But I tell you one thing they all had in common afterwards
...'

'What's that?'

'They were dead!' he laughs. 'From the time they were
thrown into the common burial pit and covered with earth
they never rose again!'

'But the other Jesus wasn't put into the common pit, was
he?'

'No, you're right about that. They say he had a rich friend, a member of the Council, owner of a stone-built tomb, and he was put in there instead. His friend must have been rich because tombs like that are cut out of solid rock.'

'Did your father know the Christians' Jesus or his friend who provided the tomb?'

'No, but in a way that Jesus rescued my father. You see, my father was in prison under a death sentence for rebellion at a time of year when the Roman governor sometimes used to release a condemned prisoner as a good-will action. It wasn't a proper, legal right but he'd do it to keep the Passover crowds happy. Keeping them happy could stop a riot, which he didn't want at any price. His soldiers were always outnumbered by the thousands of pilgrims visiting Jerusalem for Passover. All he wanted was to get back north to his posh villa overlooking the sea at Caesarea.

'They say he was looking for a way to get Jesus of Nazareth – the other Jesus – released, because he couldn't find a real charge against him, but that's not the sort of man that governor was. He was as much a thug as you'd find anywhere, only with Roman authority behind him. Anyhow, he offered Jesus of Nazareth as the release prisoner for the festival. But the crowds wanted Father instead. That's democracy for you – rule of the people in your Greek language. The people wanted Father. He'd killed Romans, plenty of 'em. That's why the people liked him! He could put away a few more!'

You're about to suggest that the people might have been put up to shout for him when a look in Simon's eye and the two weapons he's holding tell you that raising that question might not be tactful. Instead you ask: 'Do you feel sorry for the other Jesus?'

'Why should I? It's a tough world. He was executed on a

charge of putting himself up as a king. Well, he made a pretty feeble job of it. What sort of king has no army? There were five thousand in the desert with him once, but did he bring them in to attack Jerusalem or Herodium or the other Roman forts? Never! All he did was share a meal with them and send them home. What sort of fighter does that? When they did arrest him, his friends all ran off. Only his women friends dared watch the execution. King of the rats, I should call him.'

'Have you heard talk of Judas Iscariot, the traitor?'

'There you go again. One of Jesus of Nazareth's so-called friends betrayed him. I've heard that his very best friend denied that he even knew him.* The others ran away. I tell you, I've got better friends here than he ever had, poor bloke. And this is a more reliable friend than his twelve!' he exclaims, lifting his sword.

'Was Judas a zealot?'

'Who knows? We don't keep membership lists, you know. Far too dangerous. Also, zealots have never been a single, trained resistance force. We're separate groups. The less we know about the others, the better. Because if they catch us,' even he looks cautious here, 'there's a lot of things they'll do to get our secrets before they kill us. Being executed could be pleasant after that. So it's not just that I don't know whether Judas was a zealot or not. I don't reckon anybody nowadays could tell you the answer to that. But I've heard it said he came from Kerioth.'

'Did he?'

'Might have. Might not have. Who cares?' He clearly can't tell you any more.


Choose now:

- Whether to continue on the zealot raid, by going to page 48.

- Whether to set off for Kerioth, by going to page 52.

* See also reference on page 103.

47

Once you reach the ambush place, several kilometres from the city, you have a chance to take in the scene. The people around are tense, nervous, anxious to get on with it. They don't like the waiting. Nor do you. You wonder how it's all going to end. Are you taking too big a risk? Yet if you don't take some risks, will you ever find out anything? You lie hidden in a gulley between the rocks, next to Jacob.

'What's being carried in this convoy?' you ask him.

'Gold rings, linen for clothes for the rich, carpets, special purple robes from Sidon, along with the usual iron, tin, lead, wheat, honey, oil, perfumes, wine, wool, silk, spices, precious stones, slaves. Anything and everything! They come along the old Royal Highway, the main Syria–Egypt road, and branch off across country for Jerusalem. They'll return with goods from Egypt, imported ivory – Syrian elephants have been hunted to extinction – and incense from the south.'

'Will they have horse-drawn vehicles?'

'Horses can travel about forty kilometres per day, but not on these roads. Only Romans use horses a lot in our country. There will be oxen pulling carts, donkeys with massive loads, and the Nabateans will have camels, all slow moving, good targets. Flocks of sheep and horses for sale may be with them and they limit the speed. Families on the move will be travelling with the convoy for safety. All nice and slow.'

'Will they have protection?'

'Perhaps there'll be an escort, fast-moving cavalry, to keep up the Empire's pretence that it's cleared the roads of robbers and the seas of pirates. Only it can't always provide protection, because the troops can't be everywhere. But there'll definitely be an escort if any high-ranking officials are travelling with them.'

'Will they be on time?'

'It's the right weather for travel, and you know that the paved roads around here are five or six metres wide. That

allows travel even in bad weather. If they take a rest break before this climb, that will delay them.'

'Why are you attacking them?'

'Money for our work,' he seems not to view this as theft and goes on, 'but we might know them.'

'What difference does that make?'

'If we know them, we'll offer them a deal: they give us a tenth or maybe a fifth of their goods and we escort them safely to Jerusalem. If the Romans turn up while we're doing it, we pretend to be members of the convoy.'

You lean back in the gulley to wait. Looking round, you notice Julia has acquired a dagger from somewhere. But Paulus is nowhere to be seen.

Choose:

- Either to look for Paulus, by going to page 50.

- Or to leave before the ambush starts and set off for Kerioth, Judas' possible home town, by going to page 52.

- Or to stay and watch the ambush, by going to page 60.

# You look for Paulus

Your best plan is to scramble to one of the highest points above the road then try to spot people moving. The heat shimmers and you have to shade your eyes to get the best view. You can't see anyone moving, but you can see a small group of tents in the distance, between you and Jerusalem.

'Look,' says Julia, 'this raid won't happen for ages yet. We could work our way back towards the city and ask the tent people if they've seen Paulus. These zealots don't know exactly when this convoy's coming. Convoys can be days late. We've got time.'

A zealot overhears your conversation. 'Don't talk to those people. They're Bedouin – descendants of Abraham and his woman,' he adds, nodding towards the tents.

'What do you mean?'

'Our ancestor Abraham's wife was infertile, so he took her servant Hagar – an Egyptian girl – to have children by her to keep the family going. But Sarah, his wife, treated Hagar so badly that she ran away.'

'I'm not surprised. Did Hagar have any children by Abraham?' Julia is very interested since she's a servant herself.

'Yes, a son called Ishmael – the name means "God has heard".'

'Heard what?'

'Hagar's cry for help when she was being abused by Sarah.'

'What happened in the end?'

'Sarah had a child herself, so maybe she left Hagar alone then. Her descendants are our ancestors and Hagar's are the Bedouins' – that's what we think anyway. So we've got bad blood between us.'

Julia, however, sees the Bedouin people more sympathetically, so you stride down to the camp and approach a goatherd. Yes, he has seen a stranger, alone. He was moving back from the hills towards the city, not long ago. He seemed in a hurry.

Could this have been Paulus? The man didn't pass near enough for the goatherd to be sure whether or not he fitted the description of Paulus you give.

Perhaps Paulus has gone back to Jerusalem to find you. Or perhaps he just doesn't want to be part of the raid. Perhaps you should head back to the city and look for him there.

Before you have a chance to decide, Julia spots two armed zealots running towards you, waving you back towards the rocks.

'They're coming,' puffs one of them. 'Jacob told us to fetch you.'

**Hurry to page 60 and find a safe hiding-place before the zealot ambush begins.**

# You set off for Kerioth

Judas Ish-Kerioth? Man from Kerioth? *Did* he come from there? Kerioth is a small mountain town, west of the south shore of the Dead Sea. The climb into the mountains will at least mean you'll leave the blistering heat of the Judaean desert behind. It will be cooler and fresher up there. Your Jewish guide tells you the town existed well back in the days of their Bible. He says their Book of Joshua includes it in a list of towns of Judah (Judaea).

'You're wasting your time,' he adds cheerfully, once he's put your money carefully away in his leather purse and you tell him the reason for your visit. 'In Hebrew, "Iscariot" would have to be "Ish-mi-Kerioth", man *from* Kerioth, rather than man *of* Kerioth. That would change the name to Ishmicariot, which it wasn't. Unless, of course, Judas was

named by people who didn't speak the language as their first language. Hillel the Pirathonite in our Bible is named without "mi" (from), but *with* "ha", the word for "the". Your Judas wasn't called Hakeriothi, the Keriothite. So, when you compare with other people named after towns, no evidence exists to say Judas was named after this one.'

Do you follow this? You must be looking slightly blank because he summarizes it for you:

*'"Iscariot" is not likely to mean "man from Kerioth".* Want to go back now?' You must look glum because he tries to cheer you up.

'Look at it another way,' he says, 'a much more interesting question is why was Judas the only disciple to be a Southerner, from down here? The others were all Galileans: Northerners! Or couldn't his name just as well be Ish-Sychar?'

'I don't follow.'

'Man of Sychar – Samaria! The enemy country! That would account for a lot of his actions. Jews and Samaritans were deadly enemies. They had separate temples, separate priests, separate identities – except that they both claimed to be the only true followers of Moses and the Torah\*. Why don't you go to Sychar and ask about Judas there?' You ponder this a little.

'Or,' says your guide teasingly, 'Judas could have been Ish-Scortea, the man with the *scortea* or leather bag, the treasurer.' *Is* he teasing?

Julia has come with you but you haven't seen Paulus since you were with the zealots.


Discuss with her and decide:

- Whether to continue to Kerioth and see if anyone there did know Judas, by going to page 54.

- Whether to return to the zealot raiding-party, if you left before the ambush, and look for Paulus, by going to page 50.

---

\* See also reference on page 103.

# You continue to Kerioth

Nobody has heard of Judas. You enquire at the inn and at the small synagogue. If he came from here and had a family here sixty years ago, surely someone would have heard of him? There is a woman, Joanna, who's the oldest person in the town. She grew up here, married here, and has lived here since her husband's death. They say she's more than eighty years old. You ask for directions to her house. If Judas lived here, she must have known him. Your guide offers a final piece of pessimistic advice:

'What's the good of asking an eighty-year-old? They can't even remember what they were doing last week! She'll never remember sixty years back, if she's really that old at all.'

But you aren't so sure. You've known elderly people who don't remember the previous week very well, but can remember their childhood and young days very clearly. You hope Joanna can. It's getting late now so you decide to spend the night at the inn and talk to Joanna in the morning.

'Now let me see,' Joanna says, sitting back on her wooden upright chair, 'Judas. Mmm. Judas.'

'Judas Iscariot?'

'No, there never was an Iscariot here, but of course, people sometimes take names when they leave places. I didn't know any Iscariot.'

'How about Judas?'

'Oh yes, definitely. I remember Judas.'

You're delighted. At last you're going to get some answers. It's been well worth the journey. You wait, but she looks at you expectantly and then asks, 'Which one?'

'What do you mean, which one?' Then comes the shock.

'There were three.' This is not the answer you expected. All you can manage to reply is that you're surprised there were three.

'Oh yes, it's quite a common name round here.'

'Tell me about them.'

'Well, one was a tall, strong young man. His mother reared him on the best curds and honey just as soon as he stopped breast-feeding. That's why I reckon he was so strong. He worked with his father as a shepherd from childhood and carried on after his father went blind. The sheep-owner liked him because he was so reliable. But one summer, the year after the earth tremor, or was it the year before ... anyway, he got bad dysentery, really bad. The sheep-owner thought so much of him that he even got a doctor to him. No expense spared! The doctor put him on water of Dekarim – made from palm roots, you know – but that didn't work. So then he tried him on barley soaked in curdled milk. That didn't work either.'

'So what did he do next?'

'Bury him. By the time of high summer he'd died.' So you can eliminate this Judas.

'He was such a nice young man ...' You interrupt her reminiscence and lead her on to Judas Number Two.

'Then there was Judas, Ezra's son. I remember the scar on his forehead. When he was a boy he went rock-climbing, fell from a cliff and split the top of his head open. The

whole town tried to help to heal the dreadful gash in his head. He shrieked the place down. They couldn't stop the bleeding or the yelling! First they tried pouring on olive oil. That's a good remedy for most things, but it didn't work with him. Then they mixed honey with it and kept a tight lint bandage on, but that didn't work. He was still bleeding. Everybody thought he was going to die.

'In the end his parents bought frankincense and myrrh in a powder – that cost them dear I can tell you! They rubbed that in and it did the trick. The bleeding stopped and he recovered. Within eighteen months they'd married him off to Martha, Samuel's daughter. Soon after that Judas and Martha moved to Jerusalem. His remaining family here died in the sickness from the western spring about twenty years later.' Was it him?

'Now the third Judas,' she begins, 'he was different. He was my age. A strange boy, lived two streets away from where I grew up. There was no father around. He had leprosy and had to leave the town when Judas was a baby, I learned afterwards. But he named the boy Judas after our great Jewish hero, Judas Maccabeus*.

'Well this Judas was always in trouble, but he had a good mother. She'd breast-fed him for three years, as we all try to do to give our babies a healthy start. His father couldn't teach him a trade, of course, but the lad worked with an uncle.

'He was sent to the rabbi's class for boys with all the others, but he often dodged that. I remember seeing his uncle dragging him along the street to class holding him by the ear. The rabbi just smiled and quoted our Book of Proverbs*: "Those who spare the rod hate their children, but those who love them are careful to discipline them." His uncle often thrashed him, not that it helped much!'

'What became of him?'

'He came to no good.' Now you're really interested. 'He ran away just before his Bar-mitzvah. His poor mother –

---

* See also reference on page 103.

widowed and without a son. He broke his mother's heart and he broke the commandment.'

'How? Which one?'

'"Honour your father and your mother, as the Lord your God commands you, so that your days may be long and that it may go well with you in the land" ...'

'What after that?'

'We never heard of him again. He turned aside from his mother, to go to his own place. Why should we have concerned ourselves with him? It was his poor mother we had to look after.'

Thanking the old woman, you and Julia leave her house. You think about the Judas you're investigating. He might be none of these three. Or he could be one of them, but only one.

If you still need to decide which, reread your conversation with the old woman before you leave the village. Then go to page 58 and head back to Jerusalem.

# You head back to Jerusalem

A cold, dusty wind cuts across the hills as you walk. Your guide wraps his cloak around himself and tells you that this is why the old Jewish law required creditors to return debtors' cloaks to them at dusk, if they'd been taken as security against a cash loan. You can see why the people of this country wear a tunic down to their ankles and a cloak over it in cold weather.

As you go down towards the main Jerusalem road it gets warmer. Even the plants change. The thorny bushes, acacia trees and myrrh plants with their sticky gum resin give way to more trees and flowers. There are olive-trees even in this stony ground. By the time you reach the main road the flies have returned in full force. They can smell the honeycomb your guide is chewing. He leaves you, now you know where you are.

A movement in the distance makes you think it's possible that you're being shadowed, but by whom? The mysterious young man in white? A terrorist? One of the Emperor's spies? Or is it a trick of the shimmering heat?

- If you watched the zealot ambush before visiting Kerioth, hurry back to Jerusalem by turning to page 68.

- If you left the zealot raiding-party before the ambush, read on here.

You pause and look around you. Your surroundings look vaguely familiar.

'Didn't we come along here with Jacob and the zealots?' asks Julia, echoing your thoughts.

'Yes, you did,' says a voice from behind you. 'We've been wondering where you'd sneaked off to.' It's Simon Barabbas with a couple of well-armed friends.

'We've been to Kerioth,' you reply. 'You said that Judas might have come from there, if you remember?' you add nervously.

'Hmph,' he grunts. 'Well, you'd better come with us now wherever you've been.' He waves his sword in the direction of the ambush site.

It's all very well predicting when large convoys of travellers will arrive, but it's not a very accurate business. Nothing has happened while you've been away. Yesterday evening the zealots had to watch the sun sink down towards the distant hills and accept, sullenly, that the large convoy of travellers had bedded down somewhere safe and would not attempt to travel in darkness. The state of the roads, apart from the risks of robbery, means that they wouldn't travel at night. So the raid has not yet happened.

When you reach the ambush site, some of the zealots are passing the time gambling, using dice, to see who can shake winning number combinations. Some have scratched game boards on the rocks and are moving cone-shaped stones on them as game pieces. Some are playing a game called King's Move. Others are more athletic, wrestling or using slings in competitions among small groups. Others are sitting around telling and retelling stories. Some of the religious ones are praying, though you've already realized that how religious these terrorists are varies a lot.

Suddenly the games and story-telling stop. Word is passing along the lines. The convoy is coming. The raid is about to start.

Go to page 60.

# You watch the zealot ambush

From your hiding-place, you can see distant travellers approaching, many more in number than the zealots, moving slowly and with women and children. They're completely unprepared for battle. A sort of horror and fascination fill your mind as they move gradually towards you. They're coming right into the trap, like a big bumbling fly nearing a spider's web. You think of the big desert spiders waiting for their prey.

Some of the terrorists around you are clearly looking forward to fighting and perhaps to killing. It seems strange for people who claim to be doing this for God's purposes, to get the Romans out of the Holy Land. Julia has fallen silent and it seems as if she intends using the dagger she's holding only for self-defence, as it hangs limply from her hand. A tense silence has fallen on the attackers. But the distant noises of the donkeys, camels, sheep, and the children playing around the moving group are getting louder. You turn to Jacob:

'Doesn't your commandment say, "You shall not kill"?' He looks at you blankly, as if it's a stupid question.

'That means murder,' he says. 'This is different.'

You can see the faces of the travelling people. There are no Roman soldiers escorting them. They are entirely defenceless. Near the front is a large fat man, wearing a very expensive and obvious bright purple robe. He's on a donkey. He must be the leader or most important or richest person in the travelling group. There are about twelve veiled women riding around and behind him, presumably his wives or women. You guess by this that he isn't Jewish, as Jews are well known for their strict morals. One man, one woman for them!

Around and behind the fat man and his women are twenty or more waggons covered with cloths to hide the riches he's taking to be sold or delivered in Jerusalem. You turn to Jacob, but to your surprise he's scrambling away from you. He vanishes behind a large rock formation then quickly reappears on horseback. He rides onto the road and towards the oncoming travellers – alone. Another zealot notices that you look surprised and guesses what you're wondering.

'Either he knows the fat man,' says your neighbour, 'or he reckons this is such an easy catch he's going to give them the chance to surrender. He wouldn't have done that if there'd been Roman officials in the travelling group. It wouldn't surprise me if he wants that purple cloak for himself.'

You watch. There's no possible escape now for the convoy. Jacob dismounts from his horse and swaggers up to the fat man. The convoy has halted at the sudden appearance of this lone stranger. You can't quite hear what he's saying, but he's waving his arms around as if he's pointing to concealed zealots surrounding the whole convoy. An uneasy silence has fallen. The convoy can see that something is very wrong. The fat man looks helpless. His mouth seems to fall open and his eyes stare. He's like an old leather wine-skin, bulging and ready to burst. His wives, or women, are grouped around him, eyes peering anxiously from their veiled faces.

You notice a vulture flying overhead, circling, as if expecting a meal soon. Jacob draws his sword and walks right up to the fat man. Jacob drops his shield and extends his free arm to grab the fat man and pull him off his donkey. The only sound is his sandals crunching on the loose stones on the road. You doubt whether you have the stomach to watch the killing of an unarmed traveller, but nothing can prepare you for what does happen.

Almost before you can gasp with surprise or turn away to avoid the kill, two of the fat man's 'wives' have produced short swords from their flowing robes and have run Jacob through. You see the swords go right through his body, in at the chest, out at the back. He collapses, writhing, bleeding and cursing, onto the floor. The other 'wives' are throwing off their veils and producing swords too. They are armed Roman soldiers. At the same time, the cloths on the waggons are being flung aside and more armed soldiers emerge from underneath them. There could be as many as

two hundred soldiers concealed in this way. The men in the families in the convoy produce their weapons too. You turn around because you can hear a noise from higher up the road. A dust cloud announces fast-moving horses: Roman cavalry from the garrison at Jerusalem riding down to join in the ambush on the ambush.

The zealots, who have started to emerge from their hiding-places confident that they were about to loot the convoy, find themselves being chased and attacked by the Roman foot-soldiers. Skirmishes are already taking place, but the arrival of the cavalry has obviously persuaded the zealots to flee rather than attempt to fight. It's clear that the soldiers aren't bothered whether they take prisoners or just kill them on the spot. Terrible shrieks and cries can be heard. The fat man meanwhile has taken off his bright purple outer robe. He's not fat at all, but is wearing five or six leather outer coats as a protection against sword or dagger attack. It's a carefully planned defence. Zealots all around you are fleeing for their lives before the soldiers can catch them. Jacob lies still, amid a widening pool of blood on the road.

'They must have been warned. We've been betrayed! There's a traitor!' you can hear zealots exclaiming as they run. You become aware suddenly that you are now quite

alone, apart from Julia. You must look an obvious target to the approaching Romans.

'Quick!' she says, grabbing your hand and starting to run. 'They're bound to think that we're zealots too! We've got to get out of here.'

'But Paulus?'

'He'll have to take care of himself, wherever he is.'

A well-aimed spear – not quite well-aimed enough – crashes past you and hits a rock a few feet away. You stop talking and just run. You can hear the shouts of soldiers behind you in close pursuit and start to climb the hill away from the road. To catch your foot and trip up now could cost you your life. As you run, you round a corner and find yourself by a cave entrance.

It's a life or death decision:

- You could hide in the cave, although you'll risk being trapped there and losing your life. To do this, go to page 64.

- Or you could run on, just hoping that the soldiers won't catch you up and don't have reinforcements concealed over the hilltop. To do this, go to page 67.

# You hide in the cave

As you run into the cave, hands grab your throat and arms. Swiftly, your arms are pinned behind your back; hands are clamped over your mouth so that you can't cry out for help; fingers are squeezing your throat. You're choking. You can't move and you can't breathe either. Is this how it's all going to end, the search for the truth about Judas? Will it end here in the darkness? But among your attackers is one of the zealots who was in your hiding-place near the road. He recognizes you.

'They're with us,' he exclaims, 'let them go!' As you're released from what might have been rapid strangling, he explains, 'There are about twenty of us in here and we thought you might be Romans.' You're coughing and spluttering, trying to get air into your lungs.

'Do we look like Romans?'

'What do you think spies look like?!'

'Quiet, Benjamin,' hisses one of the others, 'do you want us all to be killed? If they're searching the hillside the slightest sound will give us away.'

'He's right,' Benjamin whispers to you. 'From now on, absolute silence. Because if they know a lot of us are in here, they'll not come in to get us and risk death themselves. They'll put soldiers on duty outside and just wait for us to surrender or starve to death. They've done it before.' You have great difficulty stopping yourself from coughing after the attack on your throat. Julia seems less harmed.

'There were three of us,' she whispers to Benjamin. 'Have you seen our companion? He's called Paulus.' Benjamin shakes his head and places his finger across his lips. Silence falls. You can hear water dripping somewhere towards the back of the cave, then ... voices! They're near the cave entrance.

'That's got rid of a nasty little nest of vipers.'

'I like to see the look in their eyes when you run 'em through!'

'It'll teach 'em a lesson.'

64

'Look! There's a cave here. Shall we search it?' There's a pause. It seems to last for ever.

'Nah. Let's get back to the cohort. We can be in Jerusalem before sunset.' The footsteps depart. You're about to step towards the entrance when a zealot motions you to stop.

'Shh,' he whispers, 'it could be a trap. They could be waiting with more men outside. We must wait till sunset before we leave.'

That gives you time to think about what you can do next. But what has happened to Paulus? At sunset:

- Either return to Jerusalem, by going to page 68.

- Or find a guide so that you can set off for Kerioth tomorrow, if you haven't already been there, by going to page 52. If you met the guide earlier, you may find it helpful to reread the conversation on pages 52 to 53 before continuing to Kerioth on page 54.

# You ignore the innkeeper's salute

He simply shrugs his shoulders and goes out of the room. Watch out!

You must move on:

- If you haven't asked the centurion whether he knows what's happened to Paulus, try to find the centurion now by going to page 78.

- If you have spoken to the centurion but haven't found Paulus, go to page 80.

- If you have found Paulus, go to page 82 and talk to some of the Jerusalem Christians.

# You run on

As you reach the summit, you can see that it's clear ahead. You glance behind you. Your pursuers have stopped near the cave and are standing talking right outside it. Good job you didn't hide there! They're obviously not going to bother to chase after you. In fact the further they get from the main cohort of soldiers, the more dangerous it becomes for them.

You keep jogging with Julia for some distance further, just to be sure. When at last you feel you can stop, you find the shady side of a large boulder, causing the lizards which are cooling off behind it to scuttle away. You both sit down to get your breath back, leaning on the boulder for support.

'That was close,' says Julia, relaxing. 'I can live without excitement like that.' The heat on the rocks in front of you is shimmering. It looks as if there are pools of water between them and reminds you just how thirsty you are.

'I wonder how that counter-attack was planned. I have to hand it to them – it was brilliant,' you say to Julia.

'They must have been given a tip-off. They don't have enough soldiers to send out like that with every merchant convoy. But look!' She points down towards a dry river bed, or wadi, you can see in the distance. A lone nomad woman is picking her way along it, with a donkey carrying leather water-jars to be refilled.

'There must be a well not far away. Let's follow her. We need a good drink. Then we can rest and go on to Jerusalem nearer to sunset.'

It seems a good idea, so when you've had a rest:

- Either return to Jerusalem, by going to page 68.

- Or find a guide so that you can set off for Kerioth tomorrow, if you haven't already been there, by going to page 52. If you met the guide earlier, you may find it helpful to reread the conversation on pages 52 to 53 before continuing to Kerioth on page 54.

# You return to Jerusalem

If you have already spent one night at an inn in Jerusalem, you can either reread this section (pages 68 to 71) or go straight to page 71 and make another choice.

By the time you get back, it's almost dark but that has made the walk cooler. You feel safe in the narrow streets. Even the smells, the hot grease of cooking mixed with the stench of rubbish, are reassuring. The traders' stalls have been shut up for the night. A lone water-carrier is shouting for trade, leather bottles slung over his shoulder, as he heads home. A distant horn summons soldiers in the barracks.

Julia asks directions to an inn. It has spare rooms and it has water cisterns in the Roman style. A bath will be possible later. The building is tatty. It must have been rebuilt after what the locals call the War, their rebellion twenty years ago. The original high, wide entrance door, a sign of wealth, has been plastered over and a small narrow door replaces it. The original floor must have been baked clay tiles, because some survive, but the present floor is poorer, beaten earth.

The owners are Jewish – a mezuzah prayer-box is on the doorpost. They offer you a footbath and the chance to wash your hands before eating. It is a simple meal, but the decorated wooden spoons suggest they must have been well off once. Although they're wearing ordinary camel-hide sandals with palm-bark soles, you notice a pair of jackal-hide sandals, which normally only rich people possess, hanging up.

Julia eats with you – on these adventures you don't stand on dignity and send your servant somewhere else. There's plenty of bread, the wheat bread of the better-off, with goats'-milk cheese, a couple of roast pigeons and the usual salted fish. To follow, there are honey-cakes and fig-cakes. Melon, pomegranates and blackberries are put out for you to enjoy with the meal or afterwards.

There's plenty of red wine with the food. Your host has scented it with jasmine and you mix it with water to taste.

Your host also offers you a light beer made from barley and millet. Julia asks for the Roman drink posca, a mixture of sour wine, milk and water. She finds it more quenching.

Your hosts leave you alone, with two clay lamps lit. You know that if they were really poor there'd only be one lamp for the whole house. A full stomach and the smell of the olive oil in the lamp makes you feel sleepy. You unroll the mat that's been provided for you to sleep on – your host has remembered to scent it after the last user. Then you get your outer cloak ready to wrap round you as you lie down. Your host pops back in case you want anything more, apologizing:

'We used to have wool blankets, before the War, but since then trade hasn't been ...'

'Don't worry,' you interrupt, gratefully accepting the piece of smoothed, shaped wood he offers as a pillow, 'it's quite all right.' He leaves you to settle, but you can't. You can hear loud voices outside in the street.

'There you are, thirty pieces of silver, as promised.'

'I saved you ten times that amount by reporting that attack plan.'

'The deal was thirty. That's more than most men earn in years!'

'It worked better than you could have dreamed. You've rounded up scores of them and you killed their leader. It'll take them a long time to re-organize after that little adventure – and you might get your promotion when the general hears about it.' You hear the sound of coins being thrown or dropped on the road.

'There's your thirty. No more. Don't push your luck, by Jupiter.' There's a sound of departing footsteps. Meanwhile you rush across the room to the door, falling headlong over the low table the meal was served on. You pick yourself and the lamp up (it's extinguished and broken), and stumble out into the street.

There's nobody there, but you feel sure you know one of the two voices, if not both of them. Was it really him? And him?

You can't do anything in a strange city at night. It would be dangerous to rush off in the dark when you don't know where you're heading. But in the morning you must choose:

- Either find a guide and set off for Kerioth, if you haven't already been there, to enquire about Judas Iscariot. This is the last chance you will be given to visit Kerioth. Will you be able to write a full report for Theophilus without going there? To set off for Kerioth, turn to page 52. If you met the guide earlier, you may find it helpful to reread the conversation on pages 52 to 53 before continuing to Kerioth on page 54.

- Or resume your enquiries in Jerusalem and try to find out from people here about the betrayal of Jesus and Judas' part in it. You could start by questioning the innkeeper. To do this, go to page 72.

- Or try to find the centurion and make enquiries about Paulus. To do this, go to page 78.

# You question the innkeeper

You ask the innkeeper what he knows about Judas. He looks rather suspiciously at you.

'I've heard the Akeldama story,' he says, 'and I've heard about the thirty silver pieces.'

'What about them?'

'Well, when Judas offered to betray Jesus to the chief priests ...'

'Ah! He wasn't betrayed to the Romans, then?'

'Well, the chief priests were collaborating with Rome and they set it up, but only the Romans could carry out executions. The chief priests offered Judas money.'

'You mean he didn't go and ask for money? They just made him the offer?'

'I've heard it told that way, as if he'd decided to do it anyway. The price was thirty pieces of silver.'

'What's that in your country's weight?'

'A silver piece or shekel here weighs 11.5 grams, so thirty are worth a lot. Thirty's a symbolic number too.'

'What do you mean?'

'Well, in the Torah, our sacred scripture, thirty silver pieces is the value of a slave: the price of a life. It's in the Exodus scroll*. Apparently when this Judas saw what he'd done, he went back to the chief priests and told them he'd sinned by betraying an innocent man to his death. They just told him, "What do we care about that? It's your business!"

'So he threw down those silver pieces in the Holy Temple and went and hanged himself. That put them in a mess, because it was blood-money, so they couldn't just put it into the Temple treasury. Instead they bought the Potter's Field, as it used to be called. From that day on it became know as the Field of Blood, Akeldama, only suitable to bury

---

* See also reference on page 104.

foreigners in.' You think carefully how this story differs from what you've heard so far.

Check your notes.


'So Jesus was betrayed and killed for the price of a slave?'

'Perhaps. One of our Jewish prophets, Zechariah, said something strange about thirty silver pieces.'

'Profits? I thought that was to do with money-making ...'

'Our prophets were spokespeople for God. The most important was Moses.'

'What did this, er, Zech say about thirty silver pieces?'

'I'll see if I can remember. One of the Christian gospels quotes it, Matthew's* I think, but maybe Matthew, like me, was quoting from memory because according to him it was Jeremiah not Zechariah who said it.'

'Why didn't he look it up? Why quote from memory?'

He shrugs his shoulders: 'You know how expensive books are. If they're scrolls they're fiddly to get out and roll to the right place. Besides, as kids we learned loads of the scriptures by heart in the rabbi's class for boys.'

'How come you know so much about the Christian gospels when you're Jewish?'

'I've a sister who's a Christian, and this Gospel of Matthew is very Jewish. It was written for Jewish Christians actually, and it's full of quotes from our scriptures. I've had a read at it myself. My sister tries to talk me into joining the new religion – at least once a week!'

'What did Zechariah say?'

'Let me get it right,' he pauses. '"I said to them, if it seems right to you, give me my wages, but if not, keep them. So they weighed out as my wages thirty pieces of silver. Then the Lord said to me, Throw it into the treasury, this lordly price at which I was valued by them. So I took the thirty shekels of silver and threw them into the treasury

---

* See also reference on page 104.

73

in the House of the Lord" – that's the Temple. Well, that *was* the Temple before the War.'

'That was spoken or written by Zechariah before Jesus' time?'

'Oh yes, centuries before.'

'It's an amazing coincidence with the betrayal of Jesus.'

'If it is coincidence. My sister's so keen to prove that Jesus made the Jewish scriptures come true that she's always quoting bits that she reckons apply to him. I think myself that sometimes it coloured the way those gospel writers wrote their books.'

'You mean that the whole bit about Judas and the thirty pieces of silver might never have happened?'

'Perhaps the chief priests gave him money, then afterwards some people thought it *must* have been thirty pieces of silver because they believed the prophecy would be bound to come true. I tell you this, though, one thing is sure.'

'What's that?'

'The Field of Blood. It's real, and I reckon blood-money bought it. I tell you something else.'

'What?'

'I quoted the Zechariah passage to you as it reads in a language called Syriac: "Then the Lord said to me, Throw it into the treasury." In the Hebrew text the treasury isn't even mentioned. Instead it says, "Then the Lord said to me, Throw it to the potter." Get it?'

The Potter's Field. Very complicated. You sip more wine and water and think about the position.

- You should have notes on Luke's account of Judas.

- You might have notes based on John's gospel, if you went to Ephesus.

- Now you can add notes from Matthew's account.

- You should know something about what 'Iscariot' might mean. Judas was the only disciple with a surname.

Are you forming an idea of what he betrayed and why? Jot down the possibilities you have come across, or thought of.

74

The innkeeper seems to be watching you carefully. As if to test you, he suddenly says, 'Hail to the Great Emperor, Domitian,' then adds in Latin, 'Dominus et Deus*!'

Is he a Roman spy, testing you? Or could he be a terrorist, trying to catch you out?

Choose:

- Either to treat this salute as a joke and ignore it, by going to page 66. If you do this, you risk arrest if he's a government agent.

- Or to return it by saying the same to him, by going to page 76. If you do this, you risk attack if he's a zealot.

- Or to reply, as a Christian might, 'We have no god except God and Jesus is our Lord,' by going to page 77. If you do this, you could be arrested by a government agent for 'atheism' – not believing in the Emperor as a god.

---

* See also reference on page 104.

# You say, 'Domitian: Dominus et Deus!'

The innkeeper simply shrugs his shoulders and goes out of the room. Watch out!

You must move on:

- If you haven't asked the centurion whether he knows what's happened to Paulus, try to find the centurion now by going to page 78.

- If you have spoken to the centurion but haven't found Paulus, go to page 80.

- If you have found Paulus, go to page 82 and talk to some of the Jerusalem Christians.

# You reply as a Christian might

You say quietly in Latin, 'Non,' meaning 'No, the Emperor is not a god.' But before you can complete the Christian sentence, the innkeeper simply shrugs his shoulders and goes out of the room. Watch out!

You must move on:

- If you haven't asked the centurion whether he knows what's happened to Paulus, try to find the centurion now by going to page 78.

- If you have spoken to the centurion but haven't found Paulus, go to page 80.

- If you have found Paulus, go to page 82 and talk to some of the Jerusalem Christians.

# You try to find the centurion

It's risky to be seen talking to Roman soldiers. Zealots might think you're a spy and then you'd be a target for them. On the other hand it's not going to be easy, or even possible, to find Paulus without Roman help. You decide to take a chance and go down with Julia to the tower which is the soldiers' main base in Jerusalem.

You ask the guards on duty if you can speak to the centurion. They ask you which one, but when you describe how you met him at Akeldama they know who you mean. They escort you politely but carefully to two more guards in a waiting-room or office. A scribe is copying official documents at a table in front of an empty fireplace. The room is cool, although it's summer.

After a while a soldier comes to the door and shows you into the centurion's duty room. Julia comes in with you. The centurion greets you and seems to think that because you've walked in to talk to him you're very definitely on the side of the Empire this time.

'I could see at once you were supporters of ours,' he explains, relaxing, 'and we need supporters, believe me, in these backwoods. It wouldn't surprise me if this crazy nation rose up again, following some shooting star or other. The Emperor needs all the friends he can get here.'

'Yes, yes,' you try not to be rude, 'but my servant Paulus is missing and I wondered if ...'

'Paulus? Missing?' The centurion leans forward as if he's particularly interested to hear this. 'Since when?'

'Well,' you think it better not to mention the zealot attack, 'since the day we met you at Akeldama.'

'He was quite all right when ...,' the centurion falters.

'When what?' you ask. What does he know about the fate of your servant? But before he can answer, a soldier bursts into the room. He looks senior in age, near to ending his army service time.

'I'm sorry, sir,' he says to the centurion, 'a body's been found on the Jericho road.'

78

'One of ours?'

'Yes, but not a soldier. An agent.'

'I'd better investigate.' The centurion gets up and reaches for his sword. 'Call the guard out.'

'Yes, sir!'

Choose quickly:

• Either return to the inn and question the innkeeper about how Judas betrayed Jesus, if you haven't already done so, by turning to page 72.

• Or go with the centurion and see whether what he's investigating fits in with your enquiry, by turning to page 80.

# You go with the centurion

Soldiers are keeping away a large crowd of local inhabitants as you arrive, much to your surprise, back at Akeldama. This is where you first met Jacob. In the middle of the field there is a circle of people surrounded by guards. As you near the centre you can see a body lying face down. There's a lot of blood. You overhear a soldier saying to the officer:

'He had money, sir, they say, good money, but that was nicked before we got here.'

A small leather purse is lying beside the body. It's been emptied and thrown away. The soldiers turn the body onto its back. The man has either fallen or been pushed on to a sword. It's gone right through him. You've seen enough. It's definitely Paulus. A distant saying from the start of your enquiry comes to mind: 'He was a member of our group ... from which he turned aside.'

What's happened? Suicide or murder? What did Paulus do to lead to either? Was he the Roman agent whose death was reported at the barracks? Was he one of the Emperor's spies, out to get you or anyone else who might oppose the Emperor arrested?

Where did the money they mentioned come from? Not from you as his employer! Did Paulus betray the zealot attack not out of loyalty to Rome but simply to make money for himself? You've heard him quote a Christian proverb in the past: 'For the love of money is the root of all kinds of evil'.* Was he taken in by the danger he used to warn against?

You think of the centurion's attitude towards Paulus when you met him. This money would have bought a servant's freedom. Had Paulus been tempted and made an error of judgment which cost him his life?

Or might Paulus have betrayed the zealots to save the

---

* See also reference on page 104.

80

lives of the people in the convoy? Did he act with what he thought to be Christian love to try to save lives?

Could he have been killed by robbers in this lonely place? Has he been murdered at all? Or has he fallen on this sword as a way of committing suicide? Could it even have been some horrific accident, after which his body has been robbed?

It's so like the Judas mystery, yet this body is right here in front of you. You've always thought eyewitness evidence is more reliable. But is it? Can you make any more sense of the death of Paulus than the death of Judas more than sixty years ago?

While you're puzzling, the centurion is giving orders to his men to remove the body and the crowd are being cleared away. He doesn't seem to notice you any more. You go up to him, unsure about what you're suggesting.

'This man was my servant. I'll take care of the funeral. He was a Christian. I'll hand him over to his own people.' The centurion turns and stares at you, surprised.

'I thought his place was here, the burial place for foreigners.'

'We've got other work to do here as well.' It's Julia. You half expected her to say something bitter against Paulus, but she hasn't. Maybe she was fonder of him than you thought. But she brings you back to the job you should be doing: finding answers for Theophilus. Where have you got to with the Judas mystery?


Choose:

- Either talk over the mystery with some of the Jerusalem Christians, whom you haven't really met yet, by going to page 82.

- Or, if you didn't discuss Judas with the innkeeper earlier, question him now by going to page 72. Innkeepers hear a lot in the course of their work. They're good sources for news. He might know something.

# You talk to some of the Jerusalem Christians

Although Christians are afraid of the Emperor's agents, they're also very keen to persuade new members to join them. So you don't have to enquire too far to find a Jerusalem Christian group and arrange to meet them.

'It's hard for us to be sure,' says Thomas, when you ask about Judas. 'After the War even the surviving members of Jesus' family scattered.'

'His family?'

'Oh, yes. He had four brothers – James, Joseph, Judas (not your Judas) and Simon. And he had sisters.'

'How many?' Thomas shrugs his shoulders as if to say they didn't matter.

'His mother outlived him, of course,' he continues, 'but you don't hear much about her husband. I reckon he was a lot older than her. Some say he was a widower before he married her and that Jesus' "brothers" were really step-brothers. I don't know. I've heard she went to live at Ephesus. Jesus' brother James was certainly one of the leaders here in Jerusalem in the early days and we've got copies of a circular letter to Christians that might have been written by him.'

'There don't seem to be many Christians now in Jerusalem.'

'That's right. We're mostly across the Jordan. It's safer, You don't get as tangled in zealots – who can kill you in their terrorist attacks – or Emperor worship. We refuse to take part in worshipping the Emperor, which can lead to arrest and execution for treason. It's pretty risky here. Too public.'

'Do you know what happened to Judas?'

'Not in detail.'

'We've heard several different stories.'

'He betrayed Jesus. He must have told the authorities where they could arrest him and the best time to take him.

He slipped out of the Last Supper to make the final arrangements. Then afterwards he committed suicide or else met with an accident or even illness in Akeldama and died. The only person who could tell you more about it lives across the Jordan in the Christian group at Pella. He's called Timothy.'

'How does he know about Judas?'

'Because his father was there.'

'Where?'

'There at Jesus' Last Supper. All the disciples were there.'

'Is Timothy's father still alive?'

'No. He was killed in the War in the slaughter of Jerusalem residents after the city was captured.'

Pella lies across the River Jordan and over sixty kilometres north of you, on the edge of the old Samaritan country. Visiting Timothy at Pella will take at least a week, even if you sail home afterwards from the port of Caesarea, which would be nearer than going down the coast to Joppa.

If you want to finish the case, you could return home now and discuss your report for Theophilus with Julia. You've got to try to put what you've found out into some sort of order and try to make some judgements about what evidence is reliable. Are you really in a strong enough position to offer a solution for this case yet? Since you've been away for months, will taking one more week to go to Pella matter very much?


You must choose:

- Either to return home now, by going to page 88.

- Or to travel to Pella first, by going to page 84.

# You travel to Pella

You're treated with some suspicion by the Pella Christians. They wonder whether you're really an agent for the Empire, but Timothy is pleased enough to talk about his father's role in the crucial last week of Jesus' life. He's very proud of his dad.

'There's always heavy demand for accommodation in Jerusalem around Passover time. The visiting Jewish pilgrims, tens of thousands in the old days, needed somewhere to go to celebrate the religious meal of Passover. Father fixed things for Jesus and his friends. He knew it was dangerous, so they arranged a secret signal: a man carrying a jar of water instead of a woman – clever, that! The disciples had to follow him to the upper room where my parents had got the meal ready.

'Eating in an upper room is unusual in this country, though you may not know that. We don't have special dining-rooms – triclinia, don't the Romans call them? We eat in the courtyard in summer and in the kitchen in winter. You have to carry food upstairs to upper rooms, but they stay lighter longer – some have a sort of lantern tower in the roof.

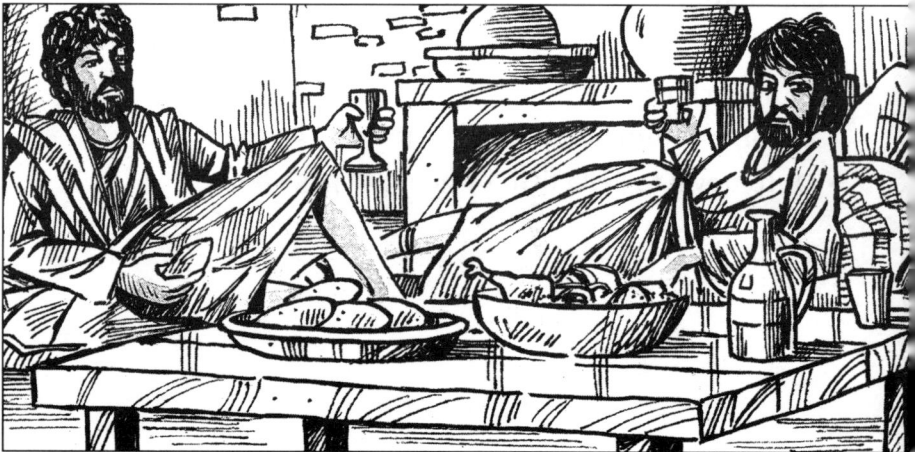

'It was evening when Jesus and his friends arrived – you know that the Jewish day starts at sunset? My father was in the room for most of the meal. He'd set out the small tables and couches and spread the cushions beforehand. It's our custom to have three people at each table with the most important table in the middle. Jesus had the place of honour, at the long side of the middle table, with one disciple either side. (Normally, the next most important person is on the right.) The fourth side, opposite Jesus, was clear for servants to serve food and drink and remove empty dishes. But all the tables were close enough for conversation and food to pass around.'

'What happened?' you interrupt. 'Was Judas there?'

'Oh, yes. All twelve of Jesus' closest disciples were there. Father insisted on serving them in person. He did it for the Teacher, as they used to call Jesus then, because the Teacher was always telling them about the importance of service and waiting on them himself. So Father saw nearly everything that happened, although he didn't hear every word that was spoken. He couldn't be near to all of them at the same time, and sometimes they talked in small groups. At other times they were all listening to the Teacher.

'Jesus acted as the host even though it wasn't his house or room. He welcomed them with the kiss of peace, saw that their feet were washed and that they could wash their

right hand – their eating hand – as Jewish custom required. He said the blessing prayer over the bread and broke it in the traditional way. That was important. There's a rabbi's proverb that says, "The person who eats without blessing their food defiles a holy thing."

'There was a big bowl in the middle of the table. They each had plenty of bread, so they could tear pieces and dip them in the shared dish in the various sauces and vegetables. But don't get the idea that it was a party! It wasn't the sort of binge the Romans go in for with their minced nightingales and dormice and bull's kidneys and booze! The food was simple.

'The talk was subdued, because they'd had a week of trouble with the authorities. Jesus had entered the city on a donkey, just as the prophecy said the Messiah would enter, and created an uproar in the Temple by overturning the money-changers' tables. The Temple had its own currency, you see, without the Emperor's head on. Coins were rolling everywhere – as you can imagine, people picked them up and scarpered! Then Jesus turned round the questions the priests asked to trap him and made them a laughing-stock in front of the people. Anyone in their right mind must have seen where it was going to end. You can't attack business interests like the temple money-changers, or political interests, like the chief priests, and expect nothing to happen. Every evening Jesus had left the city and stayed the night outside as if he wasn't ready to be taken – till the Thursday, the evening I'm telling you about.

'So you see, that Thursday night it wasn't exactly a relaxed meal. They knew there was darkness ahead. They didn't want to put their fears into words and – it seems stupid now – they were too scared to ask Jesus what he was planning. He just seemed to be going through with a fixed plan of his own.

'Anyway, the Teacher suddenly said in a voice they could all hear, "I'm telling you the truth: one of you will betray me, someone who is eating with me." They were stunned. Stunned at the idea of betrayal. Stunned that he suspected a friend. Upset in case he thought it was them. So they each started saying to him "Surely you don't mean me?" or "Not me?", that sort of reply. But he only answered, "It is one of you twelve, who is dipping bread into the bowl with me. For the Son of Man" – that was a strange phrase he used a lot – "For the Son of Man is going to his fate as it is written of him, but woe to him by whom the Son of Man is betrayed. It would be better for that man if he had never been born." ...'

You interrupt: 'Did Jesus know who it was, or did he just think that someone would betray him?'

'As I've said, Father couldn't hear everything. Afterwards some people said that one of the disciples remembered Judas saying with all the others "Surely you don't mean me?" and Jesus answering with the strange words "You have said so". They certainly started murmuring among themselves as to who it might be, but while this was going on Father was called away to fetch more wine. He couldn't allow the wine to run out.

'He was told afterwards that while he was out of the room Simon Peter whispered to the disciple next to Jesus to ask Jesus who the traitor was. Jesus gave a secret reply: "It's the one to whom I give this piece of bread when I've dipped it in the dish." He dipped it, passed it to Judas and whispered to him, "What you are going to do, do quickly." But I don't know about that for sure. Father missed it. By the time he got back upstairs with more wine, the meal was breaking up and they were singing the psalm that ends it. Father didn't notice who was there at the end and who wasn't. They all went to the Mount of Olives. Father stayed behind to clear up. He didn't know any more than anyone else about what happened after.'

Clearly Timothy can't tell you any more. You wonder: could Jesus have known who was going to betray him? Why might he have said, 'What you are going to do, do quickly'? Where did Judas go when he left the meal? Has this account made it clear what Judas betrayed and why?

You need a chance to put together all the different things you've found out or been told on your travels and to think about your report for Theophilus.

Move on to page 88.

# You return home

It will be good to be home after all this time. The overseas travelling season has weeks rather than months left. You want to be back before winter. Home seems suddenly attractive.

Before you go home, you could travel to Ephesus, if you haven't already been there, to try to talk to John the disciple. If he's still alive, he might give you vital eyewitness evidence about Judas.

• If you want to go to Ephesus, turn to page 22.

• If not, read on here.

Because you want to be home in a hurry the return journey seems a lot slower than the journey out. It gives you a chance to think about what to put in your report to Theophilus. You picture your report with four headings across the top – Impossible, Possible, Probable, Certain – and a list of questions or issues down the side – Meaning of Iscariot, Zealot connection, What Judas did, What he betrayed, His motive, How he died. You could then fill in what you have found out under the heading that fits it.

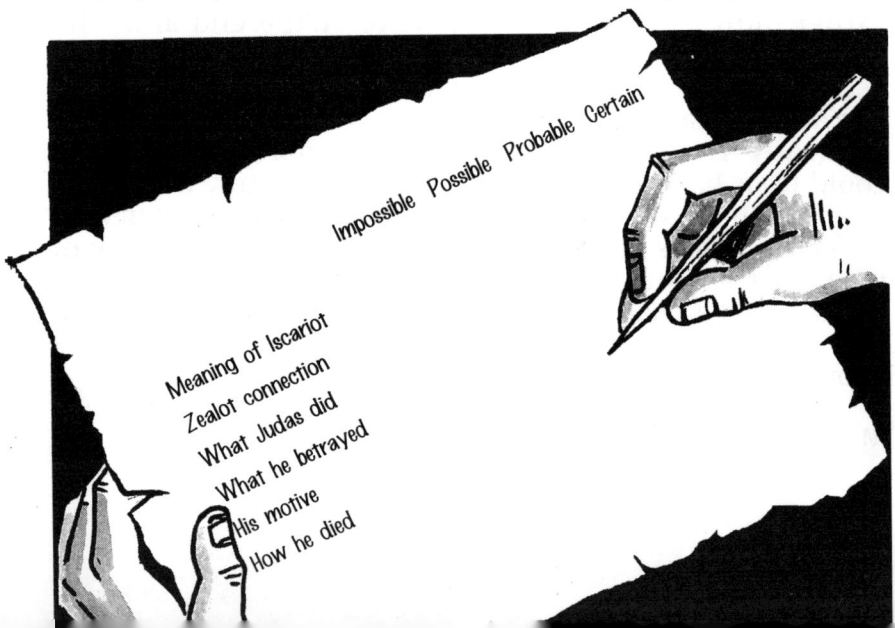

Impossible Possible Probable Certain

Meaning of Iscariot
Zealot connection
What Judas did
What he betrayed
His motive
How he died

It seems strange to arrive in your own country without Paulus. You're puzzled and sad about his death. Of course, when people go away for months at a time, not all of those who travel together always return. You can't really believe he's dead. You'll have to decide whether to replace him and, if so, what sort of servant you can afford, or whether just to manage with Julia. You discuss Paulus with Julia.

'Was it suicide?'

'I don't think so. He was killed.'

'Could it even have been an accident?'

'How?'

'What shall we tell his family?'

'I don't know where they are or if he was even in contact with them.'

'The Christian group at home will be bound to ask questions.'

'Mmm. We'll tell them all we know and let them decide the answer.'

'The neighbours will want to know as well. He was fond of the servant girl down the road. She'll want the full story.'

Fortunately you arrive home as it's almost dark, so you just send Julia to explain to the nextdoor servant that it's you back and not robbers. The last of the food that you brought will see you through until Julia can go to the market tomorrow. You sit back in the lamplight and enjoy your hunks of bread and goats'-milk cheese with cool, fresh water.

'I'd better start my report for Theophilus,' you say. Julia passes you a writing-tablet.

'That one's been reused a lot,' you complain, as you reach for your best bronze stylus. 'The wax has worn very thin.'

'I thought you'd be doing a lot of wiping out if you're drafting a report,' answers Julia. 'That's why I got out that old one. I'll fetch some parchment instead. I expect you can charge it to Theophilus – I'll get the very best Pergamum roll.'

'Save that for the final copy,' you decide. 'I've got some scraped papyrus I can reuse in the scroll cupboard. There's a reed next to it.' Julia fetches you the papyrus and reed and soon comes back with a piece from the dry ink block. She wets it and gets it ready for writing.

'You might have to sew two sheets together for the copy I send Theophilus,' you warn her. 'It could be a long report.'

'Good! If he pays well, you might even be able to afford a real seal for your letters, just like his!' she teases.

'In that case I'll be able to afford a better servant to go with it!' you reply. 'Now light me two more oil-lamps, please.'

'No expense spared for this report!' she laughs. 'I bet Theophilus' lamps are made of brass.'

'At least you don't have to polish my humble clay ones!' you answer. It's good to be home. Everything is ready at last. Julia comes and sits near in case you need anything else. She starts to doze in the semi-darkness. A draught is making the flames flicker and casting shadows on the wall. One of the wicks needs trimming and is making smoke and smell. But you're hardly aware of it. You start to write:

---

Most Excellent Theophilus,

I have returned from much travelling spent searching on your behalf for the truth about Judas Iscariot. It was difficult. The documents that survive can't even agree on how he died. Your contact Luke believed that he experienced some sort of accident or terrible illness that in Luke's view was only what he deserved, and that he was disembowelled and died as a result ...

---

To your surprise you find that while you've been busy Julia has written on the worn wax-covered tablet you didn't want to use.

'What are you writing?' you ask her.

'My own answer,' she replies, laughing, 'I might be nearer the truth than you! Shall I send mine off tomorrow as well?'

'He'll prefer mine – of course!' you reply.

'I wouldn't be in your sandals if he doesn't like yours!' laughs Julia. 'Do you want to read mine first to get a few tips?'

Now you must decide what to say in your report for Theophilus. Remember, you've been told to report on:

- what Judas did,
- why he did it,
- how he died,
- any detail you can be sure of.

If you want to go to any sections in the book you read earlier to review the evidence there, don't forget to bookmark this page so that you can return here afterwards. For example, you might want to reread the Akeldama section on pages 26 to 31 or the conversation with Simon Barabbas on pages 44 to 47.

Remember the checklist for assessing the evidence you possess:

- Is it certain?
- Is it probable?
- Is it possible?
- Is it impossible?

Think carefully about which solution best fits the evidence. Write down your answers for Theophilus, with reasons for choosing them, then go to the mirror-writing on page 93.

# Solutions

In this case there isn't a simple solution that would convince everybody. Otherwise there wouldn't be a mystery. Various solutions have been suggested at different times in Christian history.

Judas puzzled people in the ancient world as well as now and two early solutions were proposed by Papias and Augustine. In the twentieth century, two scholars who published their ideas were Austin Farrer and Eduard Schweizer.

Compare some of these solutions with yours. (You'll need a mirror.) Unlike the clues, you can read as many solutions as you like. Does anyone agree with you?

• To read Papias' solution, go to page 94.

• To read Augustine's solution, to page 95.

• To read Austin Farrer's solution, go to page 96.

• To read Eduard Schweizer's solution, go to page 97.

When you've read as many of these four solutions as you want to compare with yours, go to page 98 and read Julia's solution.

If you want to read exactly what the Bible says about Judas, you will find a list of the passages that mention him on page 104.

# Papias' Solution

Papias lived from about 60 C.E. to 130 C.E. Nobody knows anything about his life, so he's a mystery himself, except that he's described as a disciple of somebody called John (which John isn't clear). Papias became the Christian bishop of Hierapolis in Asia Minor but his five books survive only in bits that are quoted by other people.

Papias said that Judas had dropsy, an old word for the illness now called generalized oedema. The weight of the human body is roughly three-fifths water. In oedema the balance goes wrong and the amount of water increases. First there's an increase in the person's weight then visible swelling, often in the lower part of the body and ankles. It can be a symptom of another disorder. In the worst cases fluid enters the lungs and causes difficulty in breathing. Look it up in a family medical book for more details!

An untreated person with this condition might well lose their balance and fall, creating the real possibility of a bad accident such as Luke describes in Acts. According to Papias, Judas became so large that he couldn't even squeeze through a gap which a cart could pass through easily. He became blind and died in great pain.

Papias' solution has problems of its own. It doesn't quite fit any other account. Did he know something the four gospel writers didn't, perhaps from a book that no longer survives? Or did he embroider Luke's account in Acts by adding his own deductions about the nasty end of (as he believed) a nasty man?

Return to page 93.

# Augustine's Solution

Augustine (354–430 C.E.) was one of the cleverest and most famous Christians of his time. He was a professor who was converted to Christianity and eventually became bishop of Hippo Regius, where he died while the town was under siege by Vandals (the tribe who gave their name to the modern word). Augustine wrote a number of books which were so influential in Christianity that they are in print now, including paperback editions. The best known is *The City of God*.

Augustine believed that Judas hanged himself, but the rope broke so he fell to the ground, tearing himself open in the process. There he died. Because the ground was held to be religiously polluted by this suicide, it was only suitable for foreigners who were not Jewish to be buried in.

What are the problems with this view? Is it likely? Or is it more likely that Augustine was looking for a way of combining the two Bible accounts?

Return to page 93.

# Austin Farrer's Solution

Farrer's view was that there is really no mystery at all. The chief priests had no detective force or intelligence service to advise them how to arrest Jesus without trouble from the crowds. Paid informers were often used to solve crimes. Judas was one such person and simply alerted them to how Jesus could be successfully arrested.

After all, Farrer pointed out, Jesus had men with him (the disciples) who might have fought back. Indeed, a skirmish did take place in which two gospels record that the ear of the High Priest's servant was cut off. The disciples had weapons, at least two swords, so it was important for the arresting authorities to move quickly. Farrer thought that Judas was merely a paid informer.

Farrer does not comment about Judas' *motive*, which remains unexplained. The Temple *did* have its own security force (the Levites) who could have arrested Jesus on the premises earlier in the week and handed him over to the Roman authorities. But technically they had no authority outside the Temple building complex. Do you think, despite Farrer's view, that there *is* a mystery?

Return to page 93.

# Eduard Schweizer's Solution

It is possible that Judas could have been brought to trial himself for giving false evidence against Jesus, since the Christian view was that Jesus had committed no crime in Jewish or Roman law. One of the Ten (Jewish) Commandments says: 'You shall not give false evidence against your neighbour.' Faced with the real possibility of arrest and trial after the sentence on Jesus had been carried out, Judas took his own life.

Unclean money (the blood-money) was then used for an unclean purpose: to purchase a burial ground for foreigners, almost certainly Gentiles (non-Jews). The swelling/fall story may have come from 2 Maccabees 9: 5–12 in the Jewish Bible. Here the death of Antiochus IV, a Greek emperor who persecuted Jews, is described in great detail, including this passage:

And so the ungodly man's body swarmed with worms, and while he was still living in anguish and pain, his flesh rotted away, and because of his stench the whole army felt sick at his decay. Because of his intolerable stench no one was able to carry the man who a little while before had thought he could touch the stars of heaven.

There was a strong belief in Judaism, which passed into Christianity, that those who attack God or God's people will meet a just 'reward'. This perhaps shaped how the Judas story was told.

The question of why Judas did what he did has still not been solved by this explanation.

Return to page 93.

# Julia's Solution

I don't think Judas was Ish-Sicarii, one of the dagger-men, because we were told that Jesus had a disciple called Simon the Zealot. If Judas was a zealot, why wasn't he called Judas the Zealot in the same way? I don't think he was Ish-Sychar, a Samaritan, either. If he was a member of the enemy people of the Jews that would have been very clearly remembered and passed down, not just slurred into an obscure surname. So I think on balance he did come from Kerioth. Either that, or no-one has cracked the meaning of 'Iscariot'.

All he did was to tell the authorities how they could arrest Jesus at a convenient time. What he 'betrayed' was the friendship between him and Jesus. No true friend arranges for their friend to be arrested! Whether he did it for money, or whether he had some unrecorded or hidden quarrel with Jesus, in which case the money wasn't essential, I don't think we can ever know.

Did he swell and die of a terrible illness? Or did he fall, severely damaging his body, and then bleed to death? Or did he commit suicide? If it was either of the first two choices, you don't have to explain why he killed himself when his plan had gone so well, because he didn't die willingly. Not only that, both of the first two choices could be right. He might have swollen massively owing to an untreatable illness. That could have made him stumble and fall, causing such severe internal damage that Luke could talk about all his bowels gushing out. That would be another explanation for Akeldama: not just the field of blood-money, but the field of Judas' own blood. So I'm backing Luke's view of how he died and not Matthew's, even though most Christians seem to back Matthew's suicide story and haven't even heard Luke's alternative.

The trouble is, those Christians just had to make Judas out to be bad in every way. Did he steal from the common fund, or did they just assume he must have done? Did he betray his friend for money, or did they just assume he must have done? Yet however bad those Christians make him, without Judas there might have been no arrest, no execution and none of their claims that Jesus was raised from the dead.

Go to page 100.

Go to page 100.

# Your report is finished

Over sixty years since Judas died – it seems a long time ago. In years to come it might be harder still to get back into the events behind this mystery than it has been for you. Do the circumstances of Paulus' death shed any light on the Judas mystery?

While you've been thinking about solutions the lamp oil has been exhausted and the house has gone completely dark. Julia has fallen asleep on her mat. You must have slept for several hours yourself, because when you wake with a start you can see daylight around around the edge of the closed door. There are voices in the street. Next door's servant will soon have spread the news of your return last night to every servant in the street and they'll have passed the news on to your neighbours. They'll be calling and wanting to know all about your travels.

Your report must go to Theophilus without delay. Julia must go to market to buy fresh food. There are household jobs to be done. The floor needs sweeping. The lamps need preparing for the next evening. You need to check the clothing you left behind in case of damage by moths.

There's a knock at your door. Is it the first of your expected visitors calling to ask if you're inside? No, it's a young man in a white robe. He looks familiar. Hasn't he been following you on your travels abroad?

'Aren't you, er, the young man in the white robe ...?'

'There are thousands of young men in white robes. I work for

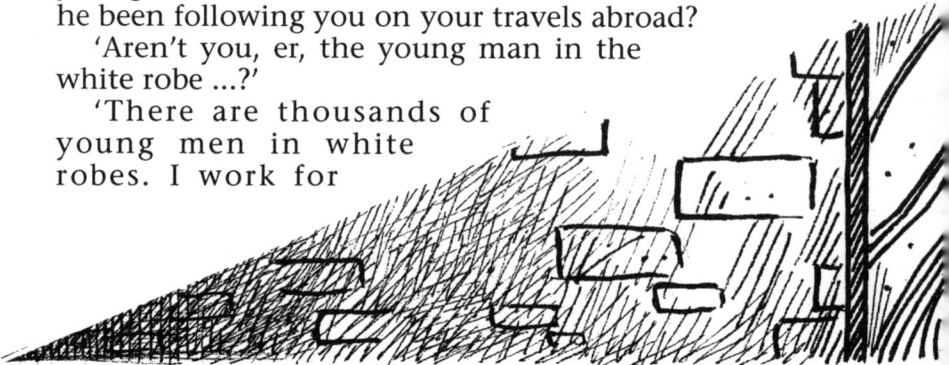

Theophilus. He wants to see you now! And I should warn you, he's not in a very good temper!'

Will your solution stand up to scrutiny by Theophilus? If not, it might be

### THE END

These references allow you to escape for a moment into modern times and read modern comments and information about remarks or events in the story.

**Page 8** Strictly, Paulus is very unlikely to have called it this. The B.C./A.D. (B.C.E./C.E.) dating system was invented later, after a Christian monk called Dionysius Exiguus, living in Rome, pinpointed what he thought was the right year zero. He did this in about the year 530.

**Page 20** A codex was a notebook, often written on four or five sheets of vellum or papyrus folded into pages and stitched together. The reader then had to cut some of the pages to open them.

**Page 24** Although we think of the Gospel of John as one book, translated slightly differently in English according to which Bible version you're reading, it exists in various Greek manuscripts, not all of which are the same. One of the jobs of professional New Testament scholars is to do detective work on these different Greek texts to try to find out which is likely to be the original version or nearest to it. Some Bibles print variations in different Greek manuscripts in footnotes at the bottom of the page. If you check one on John 6: 71 it may point out that some manuscripts say 'Judas Iscariot, son of Simon,' while others say 'Judas, son of Simon from Karyot' (Kerioth).

**Page 29** He's talking about what is sometimes called the First Jewish Revolt or the Jewish War. It broke out in 66 C.E. at the port of Caesarea and spread quickly through Israel. It was an attempt to free the country from Roman control. However, the Roman Empire easily subdued the country, except for Jerusalem, which was besieged from 68 to 70, when it fell to General Titus after fierce hand-to-hand fighting. Mass slaughter, rape and looting by the conquering army followed and the modern excavation of one house, open to visitors now as the Burnt House, has revealed fire-darkened remains and a skeletal arm from that time. Prisoners were either executed or sold off as slaves.

After Jerusalem was captured the forts of Herodium and Machaerus soon fell, leaving only Masada in the Judaean desert, which held out until the spring of 73. Rather than fall into Roman hands, the zealots there set fire to the buildings and made a suicide pact. First they drew lots to choose ten men to kill everyone else in the fortress, then casting lots again to choose one man to kill the other nine. He then fell on his sword. Only two women and a few children who had hidden in caves survived to tell the Romans the story, but the evidence of the bodies was clear. Some of the lots they used survive and can be seen by tourists visiting Masada today.

**Page 37** Possession, or in full, demon possession, was what the ancient world called mental illness. They saw that the patient was 'not her/himself' and believed that she or he had been taken over by a demon. The cure, which of course did not always work, was exorcism, i.e. evicting the demon from the person.

**Page 40** I got the idea for this from Mark 14: 43–52: see especially verses 51 and 52. I wonder if he popped back at Mark 16: 5?

**Page 42** 'Swine', an old English word for pigs, is now used in an offensive way. In Judaism pigs are not kosher, i.e. not permitted for eating, and are thought of as unclean. To be a pigherd was about the lowest job a Jew could get in the times of this story. It was how the 'Prodigal Son' ended up, until he went home (Luke 15:11–32).

**Page 43** Mars was the Roman god of war.

**Page 44** See reference for page 29.

**Page 47** This was Simon Peter, in an incident described with different details in all four gospels. He had been brave enough to follow Jesus into the High Priest's buildings, which was risky, but when challenged, perhaps because of his northern (Galilean) accent, he denied all knowledge of Jesus.

**Page 53** The dispute was about 'true' followers of Moses (and hence God). The Samaritans had their own sacred mountain, religious ceremonies, version of the Jewish Bible and even language. The point of the Good Samaritan story in the Christian Bible is that to many Jews of the time the only good Samaritan was a dead one. The feeling was mutual. Although there were no dealings between the two peoples in Jesus' day, he travelled through Samaria, spoke to Samaritans, healed one and made one the hero of his story. Samaritans still survive, near modern Nablus.

**Page 56** Judas Maccabeus, perhaps from Maqqaba, 'the hammer', fought the Greek occupying forces in the Holy Land after the

Greek Emperor double-defiled the Jerusalem Temple by sacrificing a pig on an altar to Zeus there in December 168 B.C.E. Judas Maccabeus used guerrilla tactics and the Temple was recaptured and rededicated by the Jews in 165 B.C.E. Judas died in the continuing battles for independence in 160 B.C.E.

The rabbi was quoting Proverbs 13: 24.

**Page 72** Exodus 21: 32.

**Page 73** Matthew 27: 3–10

**Page 75** The Latin means 'Lord (or Master) and God'. A good way of catching Christians out, because they wouldn't agree that the Emperor was a god.

**Page 80** 1 Timothy 6: 10.

## Bible Passages about Judas

Judas is mentioned:

- in the lists of disciples, e.g. Mark 3: 19;
- as the son of Simon Iscariot, John 6: 71;
- as the dishonest treasurer of the disciples, John 12: 6;
- offering to betray Jesus for money, Matthew 26: 14–16;
- at the Last Supper, Mark 14: 17–21, Matthew 26: 20–25, Luke 22: 14–23, John 13: 21–30;
- betraying Jesus in the garden, Mark 14: 43–50, Matthew 26: 47–56, Luke 22: 47–53, John 18: 1–11;
- committing suicide: Matthew 27: 3–10;
- dying as a result of a horrific accident or illness: Acts 1: 18–19.

These are the main Bible listings for Judas. It may help to read through them. If you are using this book in a group, you could divide up the passages among you, look them up, then report back to the full group on what each of you finds.

# Notes for Teachers

*The Judas Mystery* can be used as part of the RE programme in Key Stages 3 or 4 (S1 to S4). It aims to do two things:

- to provide an opportunity for pupils to acquire or revise background information about (a) New Testament life and times and (b) the events surrounding Jesus' death;

- to start to raise with pupils (a) some of the historical questions that surround New Testament interpretation and (b) understanding of the central role of the Bible, especially the New Testament, for Christian belief, values and practice.

Judas is almost incidental, a centre-point around which these issues can be raised, and the study of him is not – for RE – an end in itself. Historically, we have to accept that his precise role and importance are unclear. But he is ideal as a mystery figure and 'way in' to everyday life in New Testament times and some of the problems of the historical record.

Both the SCAA Model Syllabuses for RE have as attainment targets 'Learning about Religions' and 'Learning from Religion' (SCAA Model Syllabus 1, 1994, page 7) and list as appropriate skills and processes: investigation, interpretation, reflection, empathy, evaluation, analysis, synthesis, application and expression. Most of these are addressed in this book, some in depth, e.g. evaluation and analysis. Where the book is being used in group work it will also encourage the identified attitudes (*ibid.* page 8) of fairness, respect and enquiry.

Cross-curricular skills – careful reading, analysis of data and decision-making – are all required throughout the text, and although there are choices and decisions for readers to make, the text is looped in such a way that all readers will read most of the text at some point in their progress through the book.

The following are particularly suitable stopping-points for discussion between a teacher and a group or class, or by groups reporting to a class:

- page 21, before choices
- page 24, end
- page 73, after line 2
- page 74, end
- page 87, before last paragraph

In particular *The Judas Mystery* can be used:

- to introduce Christianity or the Bible in an unexpected way in Key Stage 3 (S1 to S2), dissolving some pupil expectations that RE is a predictably routine subject.

- before studying part of the Bible or Christianity in a more systematic way, to give insight into the life and times of the second generation of Christians.

- alongside work on Easter using other teaching methods and approaches.

- for co-operative work where pairs or groups of pupils work together, negotiating paths to follow, discussing options and attempting to agree a solution as they work through the book, developing group-work skills in the process.

- as an absorbing homework task which youngsters will want to finish.

- as extension work for individuals and groups, freeing the teacher to complete more basic work with other members of the class.

- as a basis for groups to report back their findings and 'answers' to the whole class or for a jury-type activity (such as 'You the Jury' in *Skills Challenge,* by Terence Copley and Adrian Brown, RMEP) – Judas might be charged with being an accessory to judicial murder.

- in RE or PSE-oriented work exploring themes such as discipleship, trust, betrayal, risk, violence (is it ever justifiable?), blame, despair (include modern religious and non-religious examples). Such discussion or role-plays by a group or class could follow the completion of reading the text or be introduced by the teacher at turning-points within it (see examples above).

Questions might include:

- Do you blame Judas for acting as he did?

- Can you find modern examples of betrayal?

- What might betrayal feel like to (a) the victim and (b) the betrayer?

- Would you feel it was unfair, or even wrong, if Judas had lived happily and wealthily ever after?

106

- Should disciples or followers be expected to suffer for loyalty to their religious leader? Consider examples from different religions or modern religious groups.
- What do you think real despair is like? How might it have been experienced by (a) Judas and (b) Jesus.
- Was Judas worse than the disciples who ran away?
- Is it likely that Judas was stealing the disciples' money? Give your reasons.
- If Judas had survived, how should the other disciples have treated him?
- Do motives matter, or should we punish or commend only what people actually do?
- Were the zealots right to use force to try to remove the Romans from what they saw as God's holy land?
- What punishment is appropriate for terrorists?
- In what ways was life in New Testament times (a) harder than life now and (b) easier?
- When you think about crucifixion, is it fair to describe the world of New Testament times as more cruel than ours?

Teachers could devise a worksheet grid for pupils based on the headings on page 88.

This book is **not** intended to replace systematic, careful study of the life of Jesus (and within that, Judas) or of daily life in New Testament times. While the writer has tried to avoid stereotyping, RE pupils may need to be cautioned to avoid making generalizations. Clearly not all first-century people would think, talk (in their own language) or behave as the ones in this story do. Care has been taken to create a realistic historical backcloth, and to introduce diverse biblical interpretations and evidence from early Christian tradition, allowing pupil choice and decision about events and alleged events. Some of the characters and events in this mystery are clearly fictitious (see page 7).

Because this book is based on evidence which itself supplies no final answers and calls for the reader's interpretation, the writer cannot provide 'the solution' at the end. Readers must attempt their own on the basis of such evidence as is available.

## Christian Study Groups

Although the book itself does not assume a Christian readership, it might be used in a church discussion or study-group context among young people or adults with the following aims:

- to introduce Bible study in an unusual and provocative way

- to provide background information about life in New Testament times

- as a Lent study base or supplement to a Lent study course

In such cases it is suggested that members of a group each have access to a copy and read an agreed set of sections before the group meets. They can then compare and discuss their answers together, perhaps using the text as a springboard for study of relevant biblical passages providing the background to each section (see page 104).

Because this book is based on textual evidence which itself supplies no final answers and calls for the reader's interpretation, the writer cannot provide 'the solution' at the end. Readers must attempt their own on the basis of such evidence as is available.

**Further study**

The writer's two books *Clues and Choices. Old/New Testament* are resources for studying selected Bible passages with groups aged 15+ and build on the awareness of questions of history and interpretation raised in *The Judas Mystery*.